The Aims of
College Teaching

role of values in teaching; indicates how teachers can aid the total personal development of their students; and shows how teaching can be made more enjoyable for teachers and students alike. Pinpointing the reason many faculty development programs fail to improve teaching, he gives sound advice to administrators and chairpersons on ways college and university teaching can be made more worthwhile—and offers practical suggestions and original insights on many other facets of college and university teaching.

Kenneth Eble has helped professors and administrators improve their skills and effectiveness in his previous books. In this volume, he reveals the new problems and challenges facing college teachers today, clearly spells out the goals they ought to be working toward, and discusses how those goals can be achieved. His encouragement, practical advice, and original vision of what the teaching profession can be make this book a valuable resource.

THE AUTHOR

KENNETH E. EBLE is professor of English and University Professor, University of Utah.

Kenneth E. Eble

The Aims of
College Teaching

 Jossey-Bass Publishers

San Francisco • Washington • London • 1983

THE AIMS OF COLLEGE TEACHING
by Kenneth E. Eble

Copyright © 1983 by: Jossey-Bass Inc., Publishers
433 California Street
San Francisco, California 94104
&
Jossey-Bass Limited
28 Banner Street
London EC1Y 8QE

Library of Congress Cataloging in Publication Data

Eble, Kenneth Eugene.
 The aims of college teaching.

 Bibliography: p. 174
 Includes index.
 1. College teaching.   I. Title.
LB2331.E327   1983   378'.125   83-48157
ISBN 0-87578-575-1

Manufactured in the United States of America

The paper in this book meets the guidelines for
permanence and durability of the Committee on
Production Guidelines for Book Longevity of the
Council on Library Resources.

JACKET DESIGN BY WILLI BAUM

FIRST EDITION

Code 8322

The Jossey-Bass
Higher Education Series

Preface

*T*his book began as an attempt to discuss some aspects of college and university teaching beyond basic teaching techniques and subject matter competence. As the chapters developed, however, they expanded into much broader considerations of how college and university teaching affects an ever-increasing number of human lives. Knowledge and its pursuits crucially shape society. Thus, what began as an inquiry into the development of style and character in college teachers ends in a discussion of the aims of higher education and a comparison of colleges and universities in 1960 with those of today.

As I was revising the final draft, I came upon an essay by Nevitt Sanford (see Whiteley, 1982) which makes some of the same observations to be found in this book. "In my more despairing moments," he writes, "it seems to me that the modern university has succeeded in separating almost everything that belongs together. Not only have fields of inquiry been subdivided until they have become almost meaningless, but research has been separated from teaching, teaching and research from action, and, worst of all, thought from humane feeling" (p. xiii). What Sanford perceives taking place from the 1920s to the present are an increasing institutional emphasis upon graduate study and specialized research and an increasing faculty emphasis on "competitiveness and acquisitiveness, absorption in narrow specialties, virtuosity untempered by humane feeling" (p. xix).

As regards teaching, what Sanford wrote in 1962 has even more urgency for teachers today: "Just as nothing is truly learned until it has been integrated with the purposes of the individual, so no facts and principles that have been learned can serve any worthy human purpose unless they are restrained and guided by character. Intellect without humane feeling can be monstrous, while feeling without intelligence is childish; intelligence and feeling are at their highest and in the best relation one to the other where there is a taste for art and beauty as well as an appreciation of logic and of knowledge" (Sanford, 1962, p. 13).

The focus of this book is not so much on what one *does* as a teacher as on what one *is*, what one *becomes* as a result of holding up high ideals for teaching and persistently working to realize those ideals. Much in this book has to do with teaching as it relates to scholarship, the relationship between knowing and making what one knows have consequence for others and for society. Running through the individual chapters and specifically confronted in the closing chapters is a questioning of colleges and universities as nurturers of teaching and learning at the highest level. This last view is not only of the universities as I see them today but from the perspective of living and working within the university for thirty years and of trying to enhance teaching and learning during most of that period.

Chapters One and Two confront closely related matters: the development of a teaching style and why it is valuable to emphasize style, and the importance of character as the necessary foundation of an exemplary teaching style. To some college professors, both matters are best left alone. Scholar-teachers develop styles of teaching as they develop styles of living. As to character, that is some kind of moralistic concept that may still have some importance in individual and public life but surely has no place in the modern university. I think teaching suffers from both attitudes. Style is not mere fashion or affectation. It is the means by which one personality affects another. As style may pertain to surface aspects of teaching and yet penetrates deeper, so character is both a teacher's inner quality and one that manifests itself to students in instructive ways.

Chapter Three continues to pursue the inescapable place of person in teaching. The analogy between sex and teaching is, like all analogies, inexact, but it suggests relationships that may lead teachers beyond workaday perceptions of the complex and personal dimensions of teaching. Chapter Four discusses the ways in which we regard teaching. Is it an art? Does it belong with the sciences? Or is it rather, as I argue, a "craft?" How are teaching and learning affected by the regard teachers have for their profession and practice?

Chapter Five confronts a major problem of college and university teachers, more of a problem as one ascends the ladder of prestige in higher education. Conflicts between scholarship and teaching are less apparent at the two ends of institutionalized higher education: at the community colleges where teaching is the dominant mission and at the established research universities where teaching is not the main priority. The middle ground is vast, and though conflicts between research and teaching vary within institutions and disciplines and among individuals, some conflicts are omnipresent and affect undergraduate and graduate students wherever they opt for a higher degree. Chapter Six extends this inquiry to question the very place that knowledge occupies in modern society. My thesis is that we have arrived at a theology of knowledge and a scholasticism supporting it which needs the same kind of searching criticism that Francis Bacon gave to medieval scholasticism. Having moved to a theological metaphor, I use Chapter Seven to set forth seven deadly sins of teaching: Arrogance, Dullness, Rigidity, Insensitivity, Vanity, Self-Indulgence, and Hypocrisy.

Chapter Eight considers how teachers learn to be teachers, and how a continuing development of teaching skills may benefit when teachers are sensitive to how human beings learn and to their own continuing experiences of learning. The focus of this chapter is on what the experiences of individuals devoting their lives to formal learning may reveal about how human beings learn. Teachers who expose themselves to new learning—not just extending their range along familiar lines but taking risks with altogether different kinds of learning—remain alive as teachers and sensitive to the demands learning makes on students.

Chapter Nine, "Teaching's Highest Aims," reflects my great regard for Alfred North Whitehead's book, *The Aims of Education*. I believe as Whitehead did, and as most educators do, that the aims of education are several, if not many. My selection of aims arises not only from my own practices but also from witnessing hundreds of teachers at work in many diverse American colleges and universities and from reading and thinking about this subject much of my life.

In Chapter Ten, the final chapter, I look back on *The Profane Comedy*, a book I wrote assessing higher education in the sixties, with a view to comparing then and now. Higher education is no less profane now, and in some respects, the conduct of college athletics, for example, comes close to being perverse. Nevertheless, the achievements of American colleges and universities are impressive and it is with those achievements in mind that specific criticisms are directed.

I think of teaching at any point in which it aspires to the higher mysteries as essentially moral, as "religious," to use Whitehead's term. Neither term is very acceptable to our time. Nevertheless, education must somehow help the individual make right choices, and somehow, too, both narrow and enlarge the possibilities for right choice. Our learned institutions bear the heaviest responsibility for social choices through which the world itself may or may not survive. No teacher can or should be entirely free from the recognition of where highly trained and specialized intelligence has brought us. Out of that recognition may arise a firmer commitment to the highest aims of college and university teaching.

Salt Lake City, Utah
September 1983   Kenneth E. Eble

Acknowledgments

*I*n the actual writing of any book, the writer works alone. However that actuality may mask a writer's debts, it does fix responsibility. My general indebtedness is great to the faculty, students, and administrators in many different places with whom I have shared many of the views in this book.

Specifically, I thank the following, though they may not be aware of just what they are being thanked for: Ed Lueders, Irwin Altman, Robert Helbling, Don Walker, Steve and Lois Baar, Lori Clarke, Benjamin DeMott, Robert and Mary Schaaf, Beth Burdett, Don Kunz, Bernice Sandler, Henry Webb, John Nelson, Dee Woolley, Betty Erickson, Michael Collins, Robert Abramson, Joseph Axelrod, Wilbert McKeachie, Dean Whitla, Timothy Bywater, Morris Philipson, John Centra, Grace French-Lazovik, Wayne Carver, John Granrose, Alan Guskin, David Riesman, Frederick Rudolph, Mihalyi Csikszentmihalyi, Alan Shucard, Hans Mauksch, and Susan Miller and friends.

xiii

I thank also the Educational Testing Service for the opportunity under the visiting scholar program to prepare some speech material that now achieves its written form; the Danforth Foundation for its invitations not only to me but to thousands of college teachers; the Bush Foundation, with whose president, Humphrey Doerman, and associates Stan Shepard and John Archabal I have been working on the foundation's faculty development program; and the American Association for Higher Education, whose board meetings always result in productive exchange. None of these organizations or individuals is responsible for what is said and how it is expressed in this book.

Great thanks to my daughter, Melissa Eble, who not only typed and retyped this manuscript but often made me accountable, word for word, for what I was trying to say. And lastly, continuing thanks to my wife and to all three of my children, who were college students while this book was being written and therefore invaluable in helping me see things from their side of the desk.

Kenneth E. Eble

Contents

Preface   ix

Acknowledgments   xiii

The Author   xvii

1.   Teaching with Style   1

2.   Character—The Foundation of Style   17

3.   The Joys of Teaching   36

4.   Craft, Science, or Art?   54

5. Conflicts Between Scholarship and Teaching   69

6. Questioning the Value of Knowledge   86

7. Seven Deadly Sins of Teaching   103

8. Teachers as Learners   120

9. Teaching's Highest Aims   141

10. The Sixties and Now   157

Bibliography   174

Index   182

The Author

*K*enneth E. Eble is professor of English and University Professor at the University of Utah, Salt Lake City. He received his B.A. and M.A. degrees from the University of Iowa (1948, 1949) and his Ph.D. degree in English from Columbia University (1956).

Eble began teaching at Upper Iowa University in 1949 and also taught at the Columbia School of General Studies (1951–54) and Drake University (1954–55) before joining the faculty at the University of Utah in 1955. He has served as visiting professor in American studies at Carleton College (1967) and directed seminars in college teaching for the Colombian Ministry of Education (1975) and the Kansas City Regional Council for Higher Education (1976).

From 1964 to 1969, he was chairman of the English department at the University of Utah, taking leave from 1969 to 1971 to direct the Project to Improve College Teaching, cosponsored by the American

Association of University Professors (AAUP) and the Association of American Colleges (AAC) and funded by the Carnegie Corporation. In 1973, he was awarded an honorary Doctor of Humane Letters from Saint Francis College (Biddeford, Maine) and was Distinguished Visiting Scholar for the Educational Testing Service in 1973–1974.

During the past fifteen years, Eble has frequently been a guest speaker and consultant on teaching and faculty development at more than 200 colleges and universities in the United States and Canada. He has served in many official positions within the AAUP, the Modern Language Association, the National Council of Teachers of English, and Phi Beta Kappa.

Eble's writing has embraced not only education but American literature, the humanities, history of ideas, and popular culture. In addition to *Professors as Teachers* (1972), *The Craft of Teaching: A Guide to Mastering the Professor's Art* (1976), and *The Art of Administration* (1978), Eble's books include *William Dean Howells* (1982), *F. Scott Fitzgerald* (rev. ed. 1976), *The Profane Comedy* (1962), *A Perfect Education* (1966), and, as editor, *Howells: A Century of Criticism* (1962) and *The Intellectual Tradition of the West* (1967). He is a field editor for the Twayne United States Author Series and coeditor of the Jossey-Bass sourcebook *New Directions for Teaching and Learning*.

In addition to consulting, writing, and teaching a full schedule of classes, Eble hikes in the mountains, plays tennis, and skis. He and his wife, Peggy, have two sons and a daughter.

The Aims of
College Teaching

1

Teaching with Style

*F*ew professors are very specific about how they learned to teach, how they acquired those characteristics that mark their teaching style. Many model themselves after powerful presences from their own student days. Some pick up hints and techniques, acts and attitudes to avoid as well as to emulate, which in time blend into a characteristic way of going about their work. Popular images of professors vary as widely as Mr. Chips and Professor Irwin Corey, selfless benignity at one extreme, insanity at the other. On television, John Houseman's Professor Kingsfield of "The Paper Chase" exercised a pernicious influence on many would-be professors inclined to bully students and to dream of the appurtenances of wealth and recognition that grace Kingsfield's stuffy malevolence. An ordinary professor's teaching style may be so conscious of making itself felt as to become mannered or may be so absent of manner that the professor appears to have no style at all. Similarly, style may be consciously acquired or seemingly arise with never a thought given to it.

1

What Is Style?

The familiar use of *style* as a synonym for fashionable — the stylish man or woman, keeping up with the latest style — casts some disfavor upon its being applied to teaching where the concern is with enduring truths rather than with shifting tastes. Nevertheless, the use of the term to denote distinctive human behavior that declares a human being's individuality takes it beyond mere manners. The foppishness that lies at the adverse extreme of singling out a "stylish" man or woman is countered by the ring of Buffon's "Style is the man himself."

The cluster of not quite favorable meanings can be dispelled if one begins with the simplest of meanings from which all else probably derived. *Style* comes from the Latin *stilus*, the sharp instrument by which we make a mark. As the most meaningful marks are signs, symbols, and words, so style in writing has a concreteness that may reside in the close connection between the distinctive mark of the writing instrument and the metaphorical distinctiveness of the writer's characteristic expression. For writers as for teachers as for artists, style is that by which they make their mark. It includes the tool itself, the skill with which the tool is handled, and the distinctive impression made. The teacher's work may only differ from the writer's or artist's in that the teacher is the tool itself, and the impressions made are on the human beings who are the direct objects of the teacher's crafts and art. Those impressions, too, like the novel or poem or painting or sculpture, have some permanence, which the act of incising makes possible.

All this is plain enough. Yet, one must reckon with a human disposition to reject style, perhaps because of the conflict between functional utility and decoration. So long as the stylus was a simple incising tool, capable of keeping accounts in a somewhat permanent form, its utility argued for its acceptance. But human beings are not ruled solely by utility. As surely as the stylus enhanced man's capacity to keep accounts, so it had within it great capacities for going beyond mere accounting. Writing, both as calligraphy and as fashioning of literature, began its move toward style, a path probably not far different from the fashioning of clothing that went beyond the basic needs for warmth and protection.

It must be, then, the overelaboration, the going beyond utility, the fussing over the manner as against function or substance, that gives style a bad name. But there is also another kind of questioning, which

Plato's philosophy established. Plato's suspicions toward art as being an imitation of an imitation are less important as a philosophic position than as a psychological one. We are not inclined to believe all we hear, all that we get secondhand — and all art, all writing, is in a sense secondhand. Nor are we even very sure about believing what we get firsthand. "What is your impression of that fellow?" someone asks, clearly indicating that an impression is something less than a precise representation, even further removed from what a person may be. All impressions come under suspicion. If one tries to make an impression, the very consciousness of the act admits of an intent to deceive. If one does not try to make an impression and yet, somehow does, we qualify our approval, for we are aware it is still only an impression. At bottom of the transactions between perceiver and perceived are the basic distinctions that Plato so elaborated: the impression, the thing itself, and the form beyond both.

Style obviously deals with impressions, and probably only those who live by making impressions — artists and writers as against philosophers, for instance — get beyond suspicions toward style. The artist is more likely than the nonartist to remove sharp distinctions between style and substance. A good writer, for example, does not have a style that he spreads on the substance of a work. Style is not cake frosting or hollandaise sauce. It is the whole thing, to be savored according to one's taste in the whole and in its parts. One can describe the elements of a writer's style, can conjecture about how it was developed, can speak of relationships between style and substance. Artists, I think, accept style as a necessary way of talking about what it is that distinguishes someone's work. Style can be seen developing and maturing both in the individual artist and in an age. And one can distinguish between style as intrinsic to the work and style as affectation, mannerism, preciosity.

Style in Teaching

Teachers, however, are not artists, nor are they philosophers, though few lack some acquaintance with either art or philosophy. Yet, as much as artists and writers, teachers succeed as they set a mark upon their work. The impression that a teacher makes lasts longer than the information that may be conveyed, endures beyond the skills that may be inculcated. As Rogers (1969, pp. 152–153) has written: *"It seems to me that anything that can be taught to another is relatively inconsequential and has little or no significant influence on behavior. . . . I have come to feel that the only learning which significantly influences behavior is self-discovered, self-appropriated learning. Such self-discovered learning, truth that has been personally appropriated and assimilated in experience, cannot be directly communicated to another.*" Reading over dozens of testimonies to their teachers from men and women of great accomplishment in all fields, I am struck by how often the details remembered are aspects of presence rather than of any specific knowledge. Recognition of the latter relates to the person's published work. As for teaching, the teacher's attitudes, values, and behaviors are what remain in the memory of the pupils.

Two examples will suffice here. One is negative (to my mind), the other positive. The first is from an essay by a young English professor, Steven Weiss (1982). Weiss attacks the excessive "caring" for students that he perceives as an indefensible current teaching style. As a counter, he offers "Max," a great Chaucerian from Weiss's Princeton days. Max was, in Weiss's memory, "brilliant, eloquent, and professorial." Beyond that, he remembers that Max force-fed him "a foul stew" of literature and grammar in freshman English. "What made Max unique," Weiss writes, "was neither his mental prowess nor his propensity to be disliked. Rather, it was his aloofness." There is no evidence in Weiss's account that Max taught him much, if one leaves aside arrogance toward students and groveling before knowledge. Nor is Max to be charged with the fact that a student found Weiss's lectures "boring, pseudo-intellectual, and pedantic," thus provoking Weiss's reminiscence. My point is not to question Weiss's judgments about this best of all professors whose guts he hated, but rather to emphasize the impact that Max made, and by the very absence of personal attributes one normally expects in human relationships.

On the other side is the example of John William Miller, professor of philosophy at Williams College from 1924 to 1960, regularly voted by the Williams senior class as the teacher "whose personality has influenced you most." According to his student, George Brockway (1980), now chairman of Norton Publishing Company: "A favorite word with him was 'presence,' by which he meant proclaiming one's thoughts in one's actions and accepting in one's thoughts the implications of one's actions. His own presence was powerful and immediately felt by all his students." Yet, Brockway writes, "He was much concerned with style, sometimes contending (falsely) that he had none."

As Professor Miller was uneasy about style, so both these students of revered professors seem bothered by any possibility that their "ideal teacher" might have had personal characteristics that had an impact. Brockway: "He made none of the usual plays for popularity. His classes did not start with warm-up jokes, nor did he make regular-guy references to football games or house parties." Weiss: "Max didn't care about his students. He wasn't worried about whether they were passing his courses. He didn't really seem concerned that most of them never expressed a passion for the subjects of his lectures. And, most of all, Max didn't give a damn how his students felt about him." Yet, both dwell upon the way each came across to *him*, and by extension, to other students as well (though we probably do not hear from those who did not pass their courses). It is precisely that way a teacher comes across that I am talking about as style, and the impact that style makes, whether it turns (temporarily, I hope) a young teacher into an intellectual prig, or an older, wiser head into seeing the play of form and substance in a great teacher's work. Nor is either professor in these anecdotes to be adjudged free from consciously affecting a distinctive style. Professor Miller, so Brockway implies, was mindful enough of developing a teaching style that he preserved several letters from a senior colleague of "ambivalently avuncular advice" on his teaching. And any Princeton professor or student knows the aura that aloofness, toughness, and disdain create, as sure a path to distinction among undergraduates as regular-guy references.

Lucas (1962, p. 47) has written that "literary style is simply a means by which one personality moves another." As simple as that sounds, and as applicable as it is to teaching, acceptance of a large role for personality in teaching comes hard for a university faculty. Certainly, professing at the university level excites sufficient personal vanities to suggest that a concern for personality is not altogether absent. And only a very foolish person would deny that we are all powerfully influenced by the personalities of those we listen to and learn from. Perhaps we shy away from personality in teaching because, up until very recently, the scientific outlook that dominates higher education still believed in impersonal, objective truth. (It is not that we have abandoned that belief but that we are coming to see the personal character of much that passes for objective truth and we are less certain of the possibility of arriving at objective truth.) Or it may be that the detached, necessarily isolated (at times) behavior characteristic of the scholar attracts to university faculties numbers of those who are, in both good and bad senses, relatively devoid of personality. A philosopher/mathematician of my acquaintance has been bold enough to say that mathematics attracts the self-contained and inner-directed and that mathematicians, as a group, tend to possess traits that as a rule do not characterize effective classroom instruction. "We convince," Whitman said, "by our presence." Given the conventions and structures and physical arrangements that shape university teaching, the teacher's personality is an important fact, undeniable in any common-sense notion of teaching, and worthy of more consideration than it is commonly given.

Presence and Acquiring a Style

I begin with these general reflections about style to offset negative reactions that often arise from giving importance to a teacher's style and from emphasizing the essentially personal dimensions of teaching. Odd, that so human an occupation should back away from its essential humanness. Perhaps this uneasiness about style begins in the difficulty of defining such essential concepts as *personality, style,* and *presence. Presence* has a spectrum of meanings, from the simple fact of being there — "we request your presence" — at one end, to some kind of spiritual manifestation — "I felt a presence within the room" — at the other. Presence of mind is a quality almost all human beings value, though it is a quality that popular lore denies to professors, not because they have no minds, but because their minds are often not present. Presence is more than how we appear, less, probably, than what we are, a compound of both personality and character. Individuals who possess presence have some assurance of what they are, and give some assurance to others that they know what they are about. Presence may be the understated aspect of style, least likely to arouse arguments about its necessity for effective teaching.

But it is one thing to acknowledge a need for presence; it is another to say how one goes about acquiring it. Presence has something to do with how a person looks, how a person acts, ultimately what a person is. But how do we look? Hard for anyone to say. Easy to deny that it has any importance at all, particularly for college professors. College teaching is a forgiving profession. Among those occupations that demand public performance, college teaching demands less as to personal appearance than any other one. A professor can be short or tall, handsome or ugly, dexterous or clumsy; though such qualities may bear upon gaining presence, none denies the possibility.

To use myself, not as model, but as example of how we may look, I had a pleasant conversation last year with a woman who had taken classes from me twenty years ago, when I was in my first years of teaching. She was an articulate, poised, middle-aged woman—had "presence"—and she volunteered what she had remembered most about my earlier professorial self. I was, she said, "a neat dresser." I was surprised, and a bit disappointed; I had expected some comment about my qualities of mind. Moreover, I am no longer a neat dresser, I have not worn a tie for about as long as many professors have not worn ties. When I was a neat dresser I had a variety of ties and suits and sport coats (some with leather elbow patches), an oversupply of white shirts, and shiny shoes. I have not yet gone back to wearing any of them, though I notice that fashion is moving in that direction.

My reasons for having been a neat dresser are as obvious as for my current mode of dress. I came out West from the East, and suits and coats and ties were what professors wore back there then. So I carried my Eastern style with me, kept it, and relinquished it as the sixties swept out "neat" in almost everything but the vocabulary. As to the present, I like to be comfortable, and besides, I flinch at the price of clothing, as I do at the price of butter and hamburger and magazines. So shabbiness of sorts fits my need for comfort, utility, and economy. It also sufficiently fits my academic surroundings that I am not forced out of a not very consciously chosen style of dress. Shabbiness has always had a vogue in academia, as if to emphasize the superiority of substance over style. ("You mean that guy in the sweat shirt won the Nobel Prize?")

But there is another side to this example. Though how I looked at different times in my career may have had little effect on my presence as teacher, it had some importance. At all times, my appearance had to have some fit with what I was, if only to free me from being ill at ease, self-conscious, lacking in presence. I could not then add to my physical height as I cannot now subtract from my sixty years. But I can, and do, bring myself to the classroom with some sense of fit between my inner and outer selves that in an important way defines my presence.

Obviously, one can work at either the inner or outer self to acquire the poise I am delineating. If you have the heart of a real estate broker, you can find the clothes to match. If an elegance of dress serves

to refine the beast within, so much the better. A middle-aged acquaintance of mine, long plagued with being an unpopular teacher, sought
help from his colleagues. What had he, himself, tried to do? Well, he had
bought a less severe pair of glasses. It had not helped much. Still it was a
beginning. Later, for more reasons than enhancing his professorial presence, he took off thirty pounds, and could wear clothes of a jauntier if
dated kind he had put away twenty years ago. That helped a little more.
He has taken on more presence among his colleagues, and I suspect
among his students.

I go on so long about looks because it is to most professors' reasoned judgment the least important aspect of their professional worth.
Nor do I wish to attach undue importance to it myself. Professors upset
about student evaluations cite the triviality of such items as "Dresses
neatly" or "Is always well-groomed." As regards student evaluations,
such questions *are* trivial. They are not to be found on respectable student questionnaires because research into the correlation between what
teachers do and how students perceive their effectiveness reveals little
correlation for questions of this kind. Students apparently both ignore
and notice how professors look. I do not think it is an isolated instance
on my campus that students in a certain mathematics professor's class
regularly make bets on how many days he will wear the same suit. One
of our best philosophy professors is remembered by at least one former
student, himself a philosophy professor now, as the one who always wore
cowboy boots. What can be reasonably concluded is that how we look
must be placed with the hundreds of other conscious and unconscious
ways we come across to our students, some of which are matters of conscious choice and purposeful development.

Teaching and Acting

Extend looks beyond a choice of clothing, wearing or not wearing
a beard, chewing a pipe, or carrying a green book bag. How do we look
in the art of teaching? Do we move aimlessly out of sync with where we
want attention directed? Do we block what we may have written on the
blackboard? Do we talk to the windows or to our shoes? Do we hunker
down, detach ourselves, sermonize? Shift the verb to can. Can we register anger? Can we show passion, demonstrate encouragement? Can we
feign surprise or ignorance or incomprehension?

If we would develop an effective teaching style, we should be able to do all those things and more, and develop the judgment that chooses when to and when not to. Teaching would not be greatly impaired by having an acting course or acting experience as part of every teacher's graduate work. For if presence has something to do with how a person looks, it has more to do with how one acts, what one does. The classroom, like it or not, is a public platform, and though that is not the whole of teaching, it is the main stage. We spend too much time worrying about the deceit of acting, too little about the impact it enables one human being to have on another, too little on how much fun it is, for both actor and audience. A feel for drama and a recognition of oneself as performer and of acting as the developed art of the performer are essential parts of the self-tutoring or outside instruction that go into developing presence and style.

More of us should attempt what a handful of teachers do regularly: go the whole way and take on, in clothes, grooming, manner, and substance, the persons about whom we teach. To be Newton for an hour or Thoreau—even in fun—is rather to be wished for than sneered at. Why should we not, at the least, step in the classroom and take on our better than ordinary selves? I am not, in dwelling on the person's being and doing, unmindful that much of the impact we make is verbal— through our speaking voice, in the verbal exchange of students and teacher, and in the writing we both elicit and make response to. The actor is a better model for how we might develop our speaking presences than the public speaker, a vastly better model than the professional scholar reading a paper to a professional audience.

Students know teachers by patterns of utterance, pet expressions, speech rhythms, and words of emphasis and organization. Eloquence is an acquired skill; distrustful as our time is of eloquence, the well-spoken person still commands both attention and respect. Teachers, who live so much by the word, should at the least, be well spoken. A young teacher interested in acquiring the rudiments of style need give attention to how he or she handles words. Like acquiring a writing style, listening to oneself and others, consciously imitating good models, practicing and refining—all these are necessary. Speaking in relation to the dramatic situation is what one might acquire by attention to actors and acting. Dramatic situations are not confined to the stage. They exist in the marvel of good conversation, even in ordinary discourse, and should certainly be part of the elevated conversation and extraordinary discourse that constitute teaching.

Acting has a third purpose in helping us acquire an effective teaching style. It helps free us from inhibitions that stand in the way of declaring what presence we have. Taking on the guise of another, we break through some of the accretions of shame and failure and hostility by which we protect our imperfect selves.

Getting in Touch with Ourselves

Last year, at my age, I found myself sitting on a gym floor in bare feet doing silly things with my hands and feet and a bouncing ball. The mentor was Bob Abramson, professor of music theory at Manhattan College, working with the Vassar College faculty at a gut level — sound and rhythm and following or not following a bouncing ball. As much as I resist the touchy-feely way to truth, I was as drawn in as was anyone else in the group, much because I was in the presence of a master performer who would not let any of us not be drawn in. What Abramson was doing, in one part, were a number of ingenious exercises in establishing patterns of physical movement and response to musical patterns and cues. He was the conductor and we were the orchestra, having only our hands or feet or shoulders or heads and, at times, voices, to play upon. He was a very tricky conductor, altering patterns, intruding into our expectations, pitting the individual's response against the group pattern, and the like. It was in this part a more elaborate musical chairs with the excitement always there of finding a chair when the music stopped and the awful possibility of being the one left standing. The other part of these exercises involved passing a ball around a circle of people, again with and against an established rhythm, and in which getting closer together was necessary to doing the thing at all.

Much of learning was there in paradigm: the need to be active, to come forth, to imitate, to perceive a pattern, to follow a pattern and be independent of a pattern, to recognize a break in a pattern, to accept instruction and to resist instruction, to set expectations and to be reinforced by fulfilled expectations, to measure one's performance from within and yet be affected by the performance of others, to feel pleasure in learning and frustration at failing to learn, to be part of a common learning and take added pleasure from the bonds such learning creates.

We were, as the jargon goes, getting in touch with ourselves by getting in touch with both inner and outer rhythms. And lest such experience be lumped with the fads of today, much of what Abramson was doing derived from the influence of his own compelling mentor, Emile Jaques-Dalcroze (1921, p. 118), whose method of music education was "based on the principle that theory should follow practice, that children should not be taught rules until they have had experience of the facts which have given rise to them, and that the first thing to be taught a child is the use of all his faculties."

I have cited only one way of acquainting ourselves with our bodies as not set apart from our minds and feelings. The physical sports one enjoys or is accomplished in afford another kind of carry-over into classroom teaching. From such a perspective, one may be able to use one's body, physical movements, to invite physical (and with it mental) activity on the part of students. An awareness of our physical selves can break into the stiffness of formal delivery, help develop a range of movement that does more than catch attention, and move us to develop a repertoire of conscious and unconscious bodily expression from the most flamboyant of leaping to facial gestures that register at close range. Without some command of this sort, style is no more likely to develop than style in writing will develop without conscious and unconscious attention to the exact placement of a word on a page.

The compound of how one appears and what one does—and with teachers certainly, what one says—results in the active presence that declares a teaching style. A mystique, maybe like the withering away of the state in orthodox Marxism, exists about the styleless style. The perfect style turns out to be no style, almost like the metaphysical conception of the unmoved mover, the mindless mind. We are back to pondering about our hostility to things, our unslaked desire for the thing itself, devoid of its thingness, and therefore perfect. To some degree, we have models for such perfection in the high degree of skill visible in great athletes, the "natural" hitter or runner or thrower who achieves supernatural results. I am not arguing against the existence of this concept of a style that has no style, nor even against posing it as an ideal. Still, I would insist that such artless perfection never arrives without a minute and multitudinous shaping of the finished behavior, without incessant practice of constituted parts, some of which proceeds out of conscious desire and active pursuit.

Studies of Teaching Styles

In pressing for respecting the notion of style, for developing a teaching style, I have deliberately set aside most of what has been written in investigations of teaching styles. For I do not want to obscure the fact that I think a teaching style is a very individual matter. "There is always something unique about the professor's teaching style, about the ways problems manifest themselves, and about the ways possible solutions can be carried out," consultants on teaching at the University of Rhode Island have written (Erickson and Erickson, 1980, p. 60). We may gain some guidance from reflecting on the details of our own practice and from perceiving the general category our teaching style fits, but we probably gain more from observing the practices of others. Moreover, formal studies of teaching styles are not far different from, though probably less enjoyable than, perceptive profiles of remarkable teachers. The most engaging of these writings go beyond the anecdotal description chiefly in trying to identify certain kinds of teaching styles.

The most basic distinction made in formal studies is that between subject-matter-oriented as against student-centered teaching styles. The distinction often polarizes discussions of college teaching and, even more unfortunately, widens the gap that separates college from public school teaching. In actuality, college and university teachers probably represent a half-dozen or more groupings in which various leanings toward subject matter or toward students could be identified. Similarly, individual teachers fit broad personality types as authoritarian and nonauthoritarian, prescriptive and permissive, doctrinaire or pluralistic, which strongly influence their teaching styles. So with labels like inner- and other-directed, leading, or exemplifying, or facilitating. More sophisticated research has attempted to identify student satisfactions with and preference for faculty teaching styles with their learning, and conversely, to identify student learning styles toward achieving a higher congruence with the faculty members who teach their courses.

One of the established inquiries into personality types, the Myers-Briggs type indicator (Myers, 1980), gives statistical verification of the wide differences in the ways individuals and groups perceive the world. Samples of differing populations consistently show, as one would expect, college professors inclining toward the introvert-intuitive side of the scale, with an emphasis upon thinking and judging, as against the general population's inclining toward the opposite behaviors, extravert-sensing. The same general difference separates professors from students and, to some degree, professors in certain subject matters — the hard sciences, for example — from those in the arts and humanities. Studies for over a twenty-year period also show general shifts within the same population, toward sensing and feeling within a student population in the late sixties, as one might expect. How valid this scale may be is not as important as what it confirms and describes in consistently used language about the differences that effective teachers have to acknowledge between their own predispositions and those of the students they are trying to teach.

One of the more sensitive books about teaching styles, Joseph Axelrod's *The University Teacher as Artist* (1973), clearly identifies teaching style as something more than mannerism or technique, though his classifications depend heavily on observable classroom practices for their identification. Axelrod's (1973, pp. 7–16) observations lead him to group various teaching styles into "didactic" and "evocative" modes, the former "designed to achieve objectives that are generally clear and relatively easy to formulate," the latter characterized by the employment of inquiry and discovery in teaching. Within the evocative mode, Axelrod identifies subject-centered, instructor-centered, and student-centered teaching styles.

Axelrod's book becomes more illuminating as regards style when it leaves the classifications themselves and turns to portraits of teachers who represent his various modes and styles. Just as one most clearly perceives style in hearing a piece of music or reading an essay, so one best perceives style in teaching by observing teachers in action or reading careful descriptions of the way they go about their acts of teaching. Axelrod uses the words "teaching prototype" to stand for "a vision every teacher holds in his mind of the teaching style he believes most effective; an image of the teacher-at-his-best. The professor's actual teaching style is the outer reality and the prototype is the inner vision" (p. 240).

One of Axelrod's (1980, pp. 7–20) most perceptive descriptions is of a "Professor Abbot," who, in twenty-five years of teaching, moves through four distinct teaching modes. These changes in his style are largely responses to the changes he senses in both students and culture but also to important changes in his perceptions of the aims of education. Professor Abbot's style may have had deeper roots than any of the modes in which it manifested itself. It might be called "responsive and responsible," "sensitive," "introspective and adaptive." To some degree, all teachers need embrace capabilities of this kind within whatever modes they practice. What I am calling for is not only the formation fairly early in a career of a thoughtfully conceived and sensitively responsive teaching style but also a continuing responsiveness to how that style retains or loses its effectiveness. The measures are these three questions: how does it fit with the students and my perceptions of their growth and learning, how does it fit with my perceptions of my own growing and learning self, and how does it fit with the highest aims I hold for education?

Developing a Style

If one's life is full of experiences and one is a good teller of tales, that might provide a firm foundation for developing one kind of effective teaching style. Further reflection, responses of students, or suggestions from observant colleagues might cause such an individual to exercise some restraint upon glibness, some pursuing of what experience cannot teach. If one has a great capacity for hard fact and solitary study and yet finds the dissemination of those facts exciting, that too may provide a basis. Better sooner than later, however, to realize that facts do not always speak for themselves and that the solitary satisfactions of hard study do not match the attractions of the swarming world that students find around them.

Simple as these examples are, they illustrate a process of recognition and reinforcing and adapting and correcting that goes into arriving at any complex and rewarding behavior. Moreover, such recognitions are a continuing process, for though there may be a center for what one does, a characteristic way of going about tasks, there must also be enough radiation from that center to catch up more students than just those attuned to a particular style. Nash (see Gullette, 1982, p. 78) calls attention to Richard Sennett's idea of "public man" as "strikingly relevant to teaching: it involves a *persona* clearly distinguished from the private self, formed in response to a common set of values and a socially determined idea of appropriate style.... Any responsible preparation must conceive of the purpose for which a teaching style is adopted, a conversation in class begun, a lecture presented. The purpose extends beyond private motive to consider academic discipline, university culture, and the nature of the student body."

As with style in art, so with teaching. One's natural bent pushed by vanity and repetition and unchecked by a sensitivity to an audience can lead to mannerisms that reduce rather than enhance impact. As self-consciousness is detectable in the manner — a carefully tutored casualness, a deliberately manufactured toughness, a feigned solicitude — so style becomes affected or precious. The sixties furnish thousands of examples of style pushed to foppery of a kind. The powerful influence of a dominant and highly visible cultural style put many professors who were beyond the age of flowering into beads and sandals and jeans even before jeans became items of international trade. In any art, including the teacher's art, style is integral to the person and that art; its visible embodiment cannot be peeled off from the outside but is there to the core.

If, as I am arguing, teaching style is not given sufficient attention, customary faculty behaviors are all too palpable in their impact upon teaching. To draw upon the analogy with writing once again, I can argue that, across a university, faculty perform about as well or as badly as teachers as they do as writers. Most — not all — faculty members can write a reasonably serviceable prose adequate to communication within the peculiarities of their disciplines. Not one in ten of that number has any distinctive style even as measured against what the discipline regards as writing well. Not one in fifty has a distinguished writing style as measured against effective prose over its long history as a carrier of thought and an inciter of emotion. The proportions are probably not far different as regards teachers. Most college faculty members have enough of personality and character, skills and techniques to teach at a level their departments and disciplines find tolerable. A greatly reduced number can be singled out as possessing a distinguished style as measured by their colleagues. And fewer still will have a style that measures up against more demanding comparisons.

Why this is so is lodged in faculty behaviors more easily acquired than style and as persistent as the bad habits of our youth. One such behavior is to gravitate to the easiest teaching load possible. Another is to move toward the best students as measured by some narrow standard compatible with a professor's reduction of life to an approximation of his own world. Another is to be guided in techniques and practices by the routes of least resistance: to favor the lecture, shun innovations and adjuncts to instruction, and reduce teaching chiefly to class preparation and delivery for a few hours a week and at the most convenient times.

Too few see teaching as a kind of day and night occupation in which one is always on call. Another set of faculty behaviors are those that shape the university in ways that can reduce teaching to its most convenient dimensions: to adopt and uphold selective admissions policies, maintain an inflexible grading system, contrive requirements and prerequisites to keep people out or flunk them out, limit withdrawals and exceptions to policies, cling to calendars favorable to the professor's work, and maintain a curriculum chiefly reflective of faculty specializations and self-interest.

I do not cite these behaviors as an indictment of college teachers. Rather, I bring them up here to suggest the kind of behaviors that may arise when there is an absence of that painstaking and loving and artful attention to the particulars of what one does — both as person and teacher. It must be acknowledged that many college teachers develop their own distinctive and effective ways of teaching without nervously watching their every move. Some may arrive at admirable styles by the route of inattention to style itself. Given a basic competence and a favorable climate in which to work and a passion for that work, a teacher may leave the development of style to the shaping and reinforcing effects of performing complex skills well. An admirable style will not necessarily come early nor remain the same through the three or four decades of a teacher's career. The highest achievement of style may come toward the end of a career in the fullest development of mind and presence that may properly be called wisdom.

2

Character—
The Foundation of Style

*T*he British scholar, F. L. Lucas (1962, p. 48), has written that no great writer has ever achieved greatness without possessing greatness of soul. *Soul*, like *style*, is a term that makes many professors uneasy. Once in a writing class when I was citing this passage, a student asked, "But what if you have a crummy soul?" My response was that she need not accept her soul in whatever condition she thought it was in; crummy souls need not always remain so. A teacher must believe in the potential for growth, of professors as well as students, of their souls as well as skills, and must try to give the student some confidence in those possibilities.

Style, Soul, and Character

But *soul* is a troublesome concept, and I use the term only as a linkage between the discussion of style in the preceding chapter and of character in this one. For it is an emphasis on inner qualities, what one is as distinct from how one appears, that marks the shift of meaning from style to character. *Character* in Greek denoted the significant mark made by a sharp object, such an object as the Latin *stilus*. Somewhat as Greek takes precedence over Latin, so a deeper meaning is attached to character, one's inner moral or ethical qualities, hence its relation to soul. In Gibbon's phrasing, "Style is the image of character."

As regards teaching, an attention to style relates to the development of character, and the notion that education aims importantly at developing character is the underlying premise of this chapter. Without character, a teacher is more ill equipped than if he or she had not mastered particle physics, Shakespeare's tragedies, or harmony and counterpoint.

Readers of this manuscript cautioned me about my emphasis on character. "It will strike many readers as terribly old-fashioned," one wrote. "Can't you find a good contemporary term? Balance, judgment?" Like Kafka's hunger artist, who would have eaten could he have found the right food, I would have used a more palatable term if I could have found one. I must use character as I have used style and bend my efforts to explain with some precision what I mean.

Lest the subject get out of hand, my attention here is limited to the place of character in teaching, both in the need for teachers to be persons of character and to assist students in developing their own. (As I write, a cat is walking across my desk, taking a cat's characteristic interest in how any object moves through space. It is part of my character that I do not belt the cat but wait out its natural disposition and let it depart as it now has. How I arrived at that choice as regards cats is hard to say. As to how we arrive at the broader range of choices that are probably at the root of developing character, the difficulty of knowing increases as choices extend past cats and seriously affect ourselves and others.) To a young man wishing to save the world, Carlyle said, "Make an honest man of yourself, and then you can be sure there is one less rascal in the world."

That notion of building character, or at the least, reducing the number of rascals, and the closely related notions of moral choice and right conduct have not entirely disappeared. We accept *integrity* and *principle* as related terms. And though men and women of character are not as identifiable on our streets as in the Victorian novel, we still can single them out among our acquaintances. The seventies were as peculiar a decade in the number of public rascals brought to the surface as the previous decade was in its number of free-floating moralists. The problem in discussing character is not with the definition but with the concept.

There is no evading the taint of goodness in however we define character. Thoreau (1973 [1854], p. 74) said, "If I knew for a certainty that a man was coming to my house with the conscious design of doing me good, I should run for my life." The right-thinking man of the eighteenth century and the principled head of family and business in the nineteenth had firm ideas about goodness—many of their ideas, by today's standards, wrong. The peculiarity of our own time in this respect evidences itself in the self-proclaimed moral majority which so exercises much of the academic community. The intellectual's hostility is in part that ancient one between intellectual sophistication and moral naiveté. The appeal of simplified moralities is as firmly established in American history as the reaction it provokes. Moreover, in the immediate present, religious fundamentalism in Iran, conflicts in Ireland, and aberrations in Jonestown commit such barbarities as to question the relationship between religion and morality. Colonialism, carried out by the major white nations in the past century, casts a longer shadow over assumptions about Christian morality in particular and the kind of character developed in Christian character-building nations and institutions.

Developing Character in Undergraduate Students

Nevertheless, we have not abandoned notions of right conduct or the idea that education might play a part in developing and refining such conduct. A teacher's character is grounded in the recognition of this responsibility and some firm anchoring of his or her own conduct as it may affect the conduct of those taught. The dynamics of that character are often matters of balancing the intellect's promptings against the whole human urgings of self and others, the abstract commitment to truth against the practical necessity of weighing and acting on provisional truths, one's professional life against demands of family and citizenship, and personal satisfactions against the insistent demands of students and institutions.

The foundation of developing character in students is their acquaintance with men and women of character. Simple as that sounds, it is the basis for humanism and humanistic education. As the university's drift has been away from human beings to things, to an examination of human behavior chiefly in terms of material functioning, so has it moved away from a nonmaterial concept such as character. Bate (1982, p. 47), writing about the current crisis in the humanities, argues that the history of liberal education in outline is the passing on of the experience of the classical world through the Renaissance ideal of humane letters. In both is "the hope of forming that mysterious, all-important thing called character as well as the generally educated mind." A further classical idea, Bate writes, was "a trust in the moral and educative effect on human character of knowledge, as the act of knowing penetrates to the confused emotion and the slippery imagination of the human psyche."

Classical education long ago gave way to technical education and almost as much for humanistic subjects as for scientific ones. The idea of shaping a human being as a potter shapes clay has been lost with it. The Greeks, Jaeger (1946, p. xxii) tells us, were the first "to recognize that education means deliberately moulding human character in accordance with an ideal. 'In hand and foot and mind built foursquare without a flaw.'" This is the ideal that operates in mentoring, that personal relationship between teacher and student, age and youth, experience and innocence, that surely plays some part in developing character.

Csikszentmihalyi (1982, p. 21), chairman of the Committee of Human Development at the University of Chicago, writes: "The main function of the teacher is not to teach science, math, or literature; it is to make being an adult seem like a worthwhile option." How strikingly that corresponds with Mentor's function in the *Odyssey*: to give Telemachus the courage to leave off being a child and to become a man. Indeed, it is not Mentor, but Athena herself who speaks to Telemachus, first through the stranger Mentes, later through Mentor. So moved is Telemachus in the first encounter that he "deemed that it was a god; and anon, he went among the wooers, a godlike man" (1.10). Becoming, even for a moment, a godlike man, is necessary to his setting out on the journey to find out about his father's fate. Mentor, before he instructs Telemachus in any way, harangues the Ithacans who have accepted the rule of the wooers, who "sit speechless, and do not cry shame upon the wooers, and put them down, ye that are so many and they so few" (1.22). Their unwillingness to choose and act morally denotes an absence of character at the opposite extreme from Telemachus's "godlike man." Athena assures him that, given his strength of character to act as a man, the means of opposing the suitors will follow: he will learn from the examples of other men faced with similar odds how to go about his task. Again, Csikszentmihalyi's comment connects the present with the past: "Of course, this modeling responsibility is not peculiar to teachers alone, but rests upon every adult member of our society. The task specific to teachers is to demonstrate, by their own example, that being an *educated* adult is a goal worth striving for" (p. 21).

It is vital, as vital as having a mentor among the louts that were despoiling Telemachus's patrimony, to have mentors among those who would otherwise dominate college and university teaching. No teacher worth the name can draw back from the impact he or she makes upon an individual student, and not just at that point of developing a skill or enlarging an understanding, but at those more important points of offering a model, standing for some ideal, and helping shape and refine choices. Our large institutions and our manner of teaching have lessened a teacher's opportunity and diminished his responsibility. Why should an undergraduate teacher worry about the model he or she sets when any one student is seen only in passing, one among many in a single class? Moreover, great numbers of teachers never see students at that crucial point of entering college or have the opportunity of following the progress of more than a handful as they leave. That fact alone has depreciated teaching of undergraduates in universities for all teachers, whatever their degree of commitment. And yet, that increases the urgency of students' encountering men and women of character, brief as that encounter may be, and not merely men and women of specialized competence.

I offer no prescription as to how we might help develop character in the undergraduate college. I do not imply that one must have creed or church or a hair shirt to develop character. Character is not built through a curriculum or grading and testing or accumulated credits inside and outside a major, but neither is it necessarily developed by a faculty dedicated to uplift. There is much valuable learning that professors best serve by leaving it alone. Character is probably built out of the play of circumstances upon the spiritual and mental and physical—let us say, in the large, the ethical—bent of an individual's birth and nurture. A faculty member develops character as he or she has principles, has moral beliefs, and the willingness to declare them. Students gain perspectives on moral behavior more from their awareness that faculty members believe in such rather than from the particular form they may espouse. The different light that a teacher's greater learning and experience can throw on behavior, however, can often affect a student's individual moral choice.

The way of valuing without indoctrinating, of granting freedom to the moral choices of students without denying them examples of supportive and opposing views, of maintaining neutrality without fostering a lack of commitment as the most desirable stance — all these are complex matters. They are better embodied, I think, than made into precept and commandment. And yet, the embodiment in a person of character would surely reveal, for instance, that there are commandments of a moral kind, in addition to legal sanctions, against murder, rape, and theft. It is bad, a teacher above all should say, to screw one's mind up with drugs, whether it be pot for fun or a three-martini lunch to swing a deal. It is bad to knife another human being, whether out of pique or revenge or to prove one's manhood or to get to the top of the academic heap. It is bad to abuse the weak, and bad to encourage the vicious. The list is long, and mounting the podium day by day to expose the world's wickedness is a compulsion teachers, like other humans, must resist if they would remain sane. Character ultimately may reside in being good and doing good, however difficult defining good may be. What may be most destructive of character, then, is not what good one does or does not subscribe to, but the denial that there is any good or that it is unimportant to search for it.

Character cannot be built on narrow or shallow experience, nor on untested virtue, nor on evasion of responsibility, nor on individual achievements alone. If it is to matter even within the small circles we occupy, it must extend itself with a vitality that testifies to the value of our commitments. Character entails some resistance to the ennui, cynicism, separatism of our calling, some standing up for what one believes as a human being, some compassion in the face of monstrous behavior, some indignation in the face of petty crime. Character manifests itself in Bronowski's (1973, p. 435) wise and reluctant measuring of the brilliant John Von Neumann, a measuring that holds that the aristocracy of intellect as Von Neumann represented it is not enough, that "we must not perish by the distance between people and government, between people and power, by which Babylon and Egypt and Rome failed. And that distance can only be conflated, can only be closed, if knowledge sits in the homes and heads of people with no ambition to control others, and not up in the isolated seats of power."

Direct Approaches to Values and Ethics

In the past, character building in a deliberate way may have been the province of moral philosophy. In many denominational schools such instruction still goes on. The closest equivalent in secularized education is the systematic work, almost entirely in the public schools, of values clarification or values education. In theory, such as that espoused by Lawrence Kohlberg, stages of moral development are identifiable much as stages of cognitive development have been identified. In application, values clarification rejects both a direct inculcation of values and a hands-off attitude to shaping values. It also sets little store by models and examples. Instead, students are presented with materials and methods that encourage them to sort out and identify their own values and to confront a variety of posed situations that require moral choice. In general, higher education has resisted both theory and practice, though probably not as strongly as have conservative groups who identify values education with the pernicious creed of "secular humanism."

One of the most ambitious and carefully evaluated attempts to develop character directly is described in a recent book, *Character Development in College Students* Whiteley, 1982). This is the first report of the Sierra Project, which began in 1976 at the University of California at Irvine. In brief, the project identified entering groups of freshmen (138 in 1976) by housing them in Sierra Hall and having them enroll in three four-unit courses during the year: Social Ecology, Moral Development, and Just Communities. These courses, as well as the work of a resident supporting staff of sophomore and graduate students, proceeded from current theories of developmental psychology, the work of Kohlberg, Piaget, and Loevinger, among others. The groups have been carefully monitored as they have gone on through college. The results thus far are inconclusive. Some gains in "principled thinking, moral maturity, and ego development" over those in control groups appear in the analysis of questionnaire data. Interviews with Sierra students, however, revealed both resistance to and skepticism about the outcomes of the project. Placed against the larger, if more amorphous, impact an entire faculty might have through a student's college career, this project's deliberate focus may limit its possible outcomes.

Colleges and universities have also been much engaged recently in applied ethics. The Hastings Center (1980; Callahan and Bok, 1980) reported that almost all medical schools had initiated at least some exposure of students to applied ethics in medicine and that nearly 90 percent of law schools had courses in legal ethics. The center estimates that there are over 10,000 applied ethics courses in a great number of disciplines at undergraduate and professional levels. As I gather from talking with many faculty members, however, skepticism about the efficacy of such courses remains strong.

Both of these direct assaults on developing moral qualities are closely related to developing character. Both may derive from the sixties, reactions to the morality of "if it feels good, it must be good," and yet some endorsement of the shaking off of conventional moralities. The moral parading of those days disturbed many professors, particularly as students drove faculty members to take moral stands on complex political issues. How acutely painful, to the extent of driving some professors away from teaching, was walking the gauntlet of students gathered to see how their teachers would cast or not cast votes on opposing the Vietnam War. Today's students press faculty very little, though at the University of California at Berkeley, ninety-five demonstrators were arrested in a protest against weapons development at the university's Lawrence Livermore National Laboratory (*Chronicle of Higher Education,* January 26, 1983, p. 2). Today's professors enjoy the privilege, as probably all humans should, of scrutinizing their moral opinions in private and of not having to take public action. A parading of character is often a betrayal of how insecurely it sits. And yet, the time to stand up and be counted may be when you are not forced to do either.

Institutional climate has changed greatly since the sixties. As a teacher's character may affect students, we are intermediaries in all times between the institution's character and life's experiences pressing on the student. I am moved still by a student who reappeared after many weeks of absence and hesitantly requested special treatment in being allowed to make up work. It was only with great reluctance that she revealed her mother's lingering death caused her absence. What struck me was the firmness with which she seemed to believe that care and concern for her mother were insufficient excuses for not completing her course work on time. She may, you say, have been lying. It might have been prudent to demand a physician's note or an undertaker's affidavit or a gravedigger's paid bill. But that is only a further exposure of an institution's character which helps create both the student's reluctance and the skeptic's distrust. What kind of institutions have we created if our students perceive in them no discounting of the worth of academic work as against the profound realities of birth and death, growing up and growing old?

Warren Bryan Martin's book, *A College of Character* (1982), addresses this matter of institutional character, lamenting its absence in the majority of institutions, hoping to strengthen it in the liberal arts colleges in which a spirit of community and a shared purpose are still alive. There is much about the functioning of institutions that magnifies the imperfections of the human beings that shape them. No single conscience exists by which to measure an institution's character. Institutions today are not the adversaries they were for many students in the sixties— bureaucratic, impersonal, inhumane—yet they have changed very little in their functioning. In many colleges and universities, teachers committed to the idea of developing character can count little on the force of the institution's character; often they will have to work against the institution's effects.

Developing Character in the Graduate School

No division of higher education should be more attentive to the character of its students than the graduate school. For out of the graduate schools come the great majority of teachers who serve in diverse undergraduate institutions stretching from vocationally oriented community colleges to eminent liberal arts colleges and from tiny denominational schools to huge public universities. And yet, graduate schools that provide the technical skills and content mastery for college teachers give scant attention to character, either their own or that of students who receive advanced degrees. The end of an emphasis on character in American higher education roughly coincides with the beginning of graduate study dominated by Germanic scholarship. Such a coincidence does much to explain the perilous civilization that followed along that path and of which we do not seem to be quite in control. I hear little enough about character even among my colleagues teaching undergraduate classes; I have never heard a dean of a graduate school mention it in any speech. I have met some few teachers in the graduate school — Gilbert Highet and Mark Van Doren come to mind, though Van Doren devoted his attention to Columbia College undergraduates — who visibly possessed character and believed in its importance for their students.

Developing teachers with both style and character is a responsibility poorly discharged by graduate schools. Except for the hiring of teaching assistants, graduate departments pay little enough heed to developing rudimentary teaching skills, much less to the idea that style and character have an importance beyond skills. Graduate schools have avoided the complexities of moral definition that create human character by accepting the single good of specialized research as sufficient to justify their existence. In so doing, they have lost most of their character as educational institutions, though they have flourished as research institutes and centers of technology.

Young teachers are susceptible to taking on the various mucker poses that can come out of the graduate school: that of abusing the authority that a little learning seems to confer, of fastening their specialized pedantries on liberal education, of catering to the paper reading, publishing, and proposal writing that builds academic reputations, of spurning any conscious effort to find out how humans learn and develop, and of disdaining anything that smacks of "education." Nor must exceptional teachers who do link style and character and mastery of subject matter be let off by their own humility before the higher mysteries of teaching. Mystery does not necessarily suffer from being thoughtfully pondered and expounded. What is most needed is a respectful and informed attention to teaching as more than an acquiring of knowledge that may be usefully passed on and more than a utilitarian task that subsidizes research.

Teachers at the highest level of formal education who are greatly involved in preparing students to become teachers have responsibilities for conveying what their experience and study and wisdom have taught them about teaching. I speak not only of techniques and strategies but also of attitudes and values and of moral choices that go into the building of character. The mentoring relationship discussed in regard to undergraduate teaching is at least as important in graduate school. As mentoring entails the strengthening of personal relationships between faculty and student, so it is as likely to enhance scholarship as to improve teaching. Graduate study is too much remembered by the hurdles that must be gotten over or around — language requirements (still having to be worked up outside the curriculum), prelims and final exams (for which sketchy guidance is given and into which arbitrariness often enters), and the dissertation (that most dispiriting of writing tasks) — and too little by the sense of a lofty shared intellectual adventure.

No graduate school is so desiccated as not to possess a number of exceptional teachers. They often include those teachers who by choice divide their time between graduate and undergraduate courses. Among them may be some identified as the best of scholars as well as extraordinary teachers. They are likely to be senior professors, for the graduate schools set much store by seniority, but they can be professors of any rank who have sufficiently freed themselves from routine to be receptive to new patterns of instruction as well as research. They are often floating faculty, some out of disaffection or boredom or expanding interests operating outside a department or discipline. Some are those whose attention to undergraduate teaching has diverted them from a research career. Always there are those who are handed the job of supervising assistants, not only because of their interest in teaching but also often because of their lack of research productivity. Many of this group are impatient with the conventional practices of the institution. Most have probably pondered education apart from the pursuit of advanced degrees in their specialized field. And most would understand what Werner Jaeger (1946, p. 28) is talking about when he perceives the "internal conflict between blind passion and higher insight" is the truest and deepest problem of all education.

The responsibility graduate departments might take on does not even require a formal program that embraces mentoring, but a removal of some inhibitions, the encouraging of some natural inclinations, and at most the sanctioning and valuing of mentoring. Baldwin and Blackburn's (1981, p. 610) studies of how faculty members develop identify "certain roles where veteran professors can be particularly effective. Perhaps a senior, exemplary teacher in each department could act as a mentor or consultant on teaching to beginning and adjunct faculty." Every graduate student deserves to have such a mentor, and if we must institutionalize it *into* the graduate program, it is because so much has been institutionalized *out*. Such mentors would not be primarily engaged in the conduct of seminars or supervision of theses, but freed to function as themselves, or as their better selves which a consciousness of their calling would call forth. The two to six years which a Ph.D. candidate spends in graduate school is sufficient to permit some minimum of personal mentorship for all students in addition to that which already takes place for some fortunate few.

I do not have much hope that graduate schools will respond either to the spirit or letter of what I have just described. They have been largely unresponsive to the recommendations for reforms coming from two prestigious commissions, one headed by Frank Newman ("Newman Unit's Report..., 1973), the other by Boyd Page (1973), in the last decade. I acknowledge the obvious impracticality of the mentoring proposal, with such awesome responsibility. But all of formal education is beset with the mentality that thinks only of measures that must apply to *all* pupils, responsibilities that must fall to *all* faculty. The only requirements for such mentors as I am describing is that they must be men and women of good character — surely some portion of a graduate faculty should qualify on these grounds — and must exemplify and be interested in the higher expanses of teaching. Doubtless, mentoring relationships would have to be built into requirements, for everything deemed of value in the graduate program is so designated. Such a requirement would probably become a mere hurdle for some students, but at least it would be a human hurdle rather than an institutional one.

Breadth and Depth

Examining once again the conflicting claims of breadth and depth is another way of moving graduate study to embrace both a wider and deeper conception of teaching. Breadth and depth are as vital as freedom and discipline in acquiring an education. Breadth and depth, however, are not mutually exclusive. Learning stretched over any period of years probably reveals periods of intense concentration on the single thing and other periods in which one ranges broadly through a vastness of knowledge that will be sampled at best. For teachers, breadth may well be more important than depth. For it is through breadth that one can provide contexts that connect with the small learning that students often possess. It is through breadth that an acquaintance with how humans learn and how one human makes an impact on another becomes a part of the teacher's learning. In the context in which I am now writing, it is breadth of experience that relates to the development of both style and character.

Reasonable argument is not likely to divert graduate schools from their emphasis upon specialization. All other reasons set aside, there is still the compelling one that graduate students are primarily being trained to fit specialized job categories. Precisely because of this strong tendency, it is necessary to argue the case for continuing general education in graduate work. If individual disciplines are alarmed by the increase of knowledge within their fields, how much more alarming should it be that all knowledge has similarly expanded. A general education that in 1920 might have seemed reasonable to encompass within the four years of an undergraduate degree may seem to be little more than a gesture today. Just as the tendency of students is to extend their career education into graduate work, so general studies begun as an undergraduate should be continued in the pursuit of advanced degrees.

But there is a more important reason, set forth by Bronowski (1973, p. 432) as "the business of science" — not to "inherit the earth, but to inherit the moral imagination." "Our actions as adults," he amplifies later on, "as decision makers, as human beings, are mediated by values, which I interpret as general strategies in which we balance opposing impulses" (p. 436). The moral imagination must not be left aside in graduate study; bad enough that imagination itself has been often held in check by the graduate school's narrowness of view. The moral imagination has as clear a subject matter as nuclear physics — the choices human beings make and have made over matters by which human beings prosper or decline, civilizations rise and fall. These choices are embodied in the lives of men and women of character. Every discipline, for example, has its great figures, the study of whose lives amid the choices they have faced is as interesting and vital as their work. How incomplete is an astronomer's education who does not know Galileo intimately, and not only as he may have encountered him so early as to draw him to astronomy in the first place, but as he now sees him from a later perspective and as he might be guided by him the rest of his life? Substitute Darwin or Montaigne or Robert Oppenheimer or Samuel Johnson. Our lives are not long enough to absorb any but a small part of those who in their own character have molded the human character.

A structure for such study is as easy to envision as a content. The graduate seminar, often badly taught and badly received, could find no better reasons for gathering and discussing than pondering great lives and great achievements. If more current purpose is desired, if we must put the immediate thing before our students to increase their willingess to explore the past, then what great subjects do we live among — and ignore — even as our specialized studies concern themselves with minute parts. Recently, Adele Smith Simmons (1982), president of Hampshire College, noted that "college faculty members and administrators... are beginning to think — and to encourage undergraduates to think — about war, peace, and the future of the world." Why should not graduate students also think about such fundamental matters? "Everything we intend to teach students through general education," Simmons continues, "to challenge basic assumptions and reach their own conclusions, to think analytically and critically, to approach a new question or area of knowledge without fear, to look at an issue from many points of view, and to be active participants in their education — can be approached through the study of peace and war." This description of what we are trying to teach is as appropriate for the graduate as for the undergraduate student. Without the inclination of graduate students to have their learning bear upon such matters, we cannot hope to arrive at undergraduate teachers with the character that will give an actual commitment to vital kinds of interdisciplinary study.

The university seminars at Columbia offer a very successful kind of model which could be made integral to graduate study. The Columbia model draws upon the faculty of the graduate school but embraces the surrounding New York City community as well. Operating outside the university, the Columbia seminars could be broad in their concerns, catholic in the participants they attracted, and could draw on the diverse resources available in New York City and to a university of Columbia's stature. Almost any major graduate school occupies a larger community that would make the creation of such seminars possible. Perhaps professors, like students, have to be freed from the tyranny of graduate work before they can operate freely as thinking human beings.

At the master's level, over sixty schools by now have created a new kind of master's degree that embraces liberal studies. The programs aim at the growing number of adults, many with graduate and professional degrees, who want to continue formal schooling but not under the constraints imposed by conventional M.A. and Ph.D. programs. What these programs have proved is the validity of such broad programs. What is given up in specialized study is restored in placing specialized competence and experience in relation to questions of great importance.

These may involve, for example, values and ethics, public policy and social concerns, and international relations. Replacing the emphasis on solitary inquiry is one on working with and learning from others. Unfortunately, such programs miss one group of students they might serve very well: students already enrolled in specific degree programs leading to teaching positions in public schools, colleges, and universities. In time, some Ph.D. programs may be affected in their practices and contents by such successful ventures as the Columbia seminars and liberal studies M.A. programs. However, directors of Ph.D. studies may find the existence of alternative programs another reason for making their own programs more narrow.

Values in the Graduate School

The university at large has difficulty in facing questions as to the relative worth of much of what it is doing. Such questions do continually arise and are often resolved by expediency and drift and pique more than by carefully considered decisions. Financial exigencies today have given concreteness to many of these questions. Some administrators and faculty are being forced to decide that this program is more valuable than that, that a whole department may not be valuable enough to maintain. Even so, the tendency is to trim rather than cut, to assume that everything that goes on within established departments is equally valuable, and to get rid of peripheral activities unprotected by departmental status. To be sure, a valuing of sorts goes on. One can see it in economic terms in the relative salaries paid to professors in medicine, engineering, education, and the humanities, for example. One faces it in the collective prejudices of much of a faculty against "education."

Perhaps, as with trying to arrive at a rational society, human beings can do no better. Our institutions are erected on the basis of what a society values; the structures that emerge reflect the values that give them public support as well as the values of those who create the interior design. Still, changing circumstances change values, and institutions change because of changes in values taking place both inside and outside the institution.

Right now, the university stands at the center of responsibility for keeping the world habitable, precisely because it was the university that placed the power to destroy the world in our hands. In a less dramatic way, genetic research has aroused similar large public moral questions. The university is not value free; it cannot be value free and the world survive. Nor has much of its pursuit of knowledge ever been value free. War and public policy and huge sums of money did vastly more to bring nuclear power into being than did the disinterested free play of the human mind.

These are such great and awful matters as to numb efforts to understand and evaluate them. Still, the efforts must be made, publicly and within the university itself. The graduate school should lead in that effort, for the values of advanced specialized study dominate all higher education. The university president whose university lives on the fruits of war does carry a greater responsibility than the president who tries to keep the liberal arts alive in some small denominational college. The nuclear physicist's hands are bloodier than those of the classicist. The graduate dean seeing only that enough research grants keep coming in to support the enterprise is a villain of sorts, for all he wears a three-piece suit and claims to have no real power.

Every teacher, as he or she would aspire to great teaching, has the responsibility to weigh and be heard in these matters. More, surely, should develop the character that turns them away from all patently destructive research or its application. Graduate school seminars need confront value questions of the weightiest kind, and not even in the familiar graduate study pattern of finding publishable solutions to specific problems. Rather, the overriding aim should be to sensitize those who as teachers and researchers have a chance to sensitize others in a common search — not for knowledge of things, but for ways of keeping this world alive and satisfying for large numbers of its inhabitants.

For the teacher just beginning in these times, these larger value questions are probably less pressing than the smaller one: what is the place of a teacher's values in the classroom? (See Collins, 1983; Parr, 1982.) Again, graduate study should give guidance, both by example and precept. The guidance most commonly offered derives from the objectivity attached to scientific research: the teacher's values are to be rigorously excluded from teaching just as they are in his pursuit of specialized truth. Such guidance is worse than none, and hypocritical beside, for the assertion itself arises out of values of a very definite kind. Better to begin confronting the complexities of the question by acknowledging the simple truth that there is no way teachers can avoid declaring values short of denying their existence as persons. The very act of showing up with a subject matter in hand, on time or late as the case may be, the clothes one wears, the words one uses, are freighted with values. But, I hear someone say, these personally embodied values are not at issue. The important questions arise from a teacher's point of view on controversial subjects, value judgments that go beyond what one's subject matter studies can support.

A recent illustration that comes to mind is a faculty discussion I participated in about values in teaching the humanities. At one point the discussion focused on how to teach Shakespeare, and a ferocious young Shakespearean challenged a colleague about his teaching of *King Lear.* "You mean," he said, "that you use *King Lear* to teach kids to be good to their parents!?" The question was a naked betrayal of how graduate education separates itself from the realities of kids and parents but also of how it makes amorality a cardinal virtue. For it is not that one teaches about a piece of literature or a scientific investigation in terms of how it defines or should define human conduct. But it is that such human questions, including moral questions, as are raised in a literary text or in a scientific study are questions of high importance. To leave such questions out of the teaching of *King Lear* — how children treat their parents, how youth relates to age, how power once given is not easily relinquished, how love and hate can drive us mad — would leave the play barren indeed. While a spate of books come forth from university presses on semiotics, structuralism, and deconstruction — the current preoccupations of literary study — only occasionally does a book appear such as Susan Parr's *The Moral of the Story: Literature, Values, and American Education* (1982).

Character in the University

Finally, if character is going to become a large part of our faculty competence, the university will have to alter in substantial ways. It will have to confront, for example, the large part it plays in sustaining the excesses of a consuming society and to consider more carefully its own practices with respect to racial and sexual justice and equality.

Once universities lived in fair austerity as compared with other institutions. Many small private colleges still do. Increasing public support and swelling enrollments of the sixties, ties with high technology, military spending, and government agencies have altered the universities' style of living. Many have become the equal of corporations in their public role, in their attention to display and public relations, and in an overall preoccupation with that which can be consumed. In their encouragement of the good life by expanding consumers' wants, the universities have created many of the strains that now beset industrial societies poised against the rest of the world.

As to racial and sexual justice, though university graduates fill the ranks of activists in both causes, the university has yielded but little to the breaking down of stereotypes or even to a marked shift in numbers of minority scholars or women in prestigious departments and ranks (Chronicle of Higher Education, February 3, 1982, p. 4). White men continue to outnumber women and minority-group members in administrative positions by more than three to one. Masculine faculties—engineering, chemistry, mathematics, physics—are still masculine faculties. Women's departments are still nursing and social work and home economics (now tellingly disguised as consumer studies). Hiring practices and promotions policies have changed very little, and only then because of pressure from national legislation. If anything, as regards race, the university appears more muddled than it was three decades ago. Back then, football and basketball teams were not predominantly black, as now, even in predominantly white universities. Today, wealthy white alumni provide the bulk of under-the-table support for black mercenaries. Increasing numbers of these do not become college graduates but rather raw material for professional athletics supported by white entrepreneurs. Wherever a racial group has conspicuous amounts of money, recently in the Arab countries, colleges and universities quickly come forward with whatever kind of academic program can lay claim to it. Ethnic Studies, however, still have not been fully accepted, much less enjoyed full and active participation from both white and nonwhite students and faculty.

In that upward mobility that promised equality if we all could get semirich together, the university still plays a part. However, often the opportunity may be there; the actuality is not. The prestige colleges, though they have increased recruiting and support of minority students, still sort out primarily from the affluent and privileged, the rising costs operating as a finer filter than ever before. The community colleges are the best that can be offered to the homebound and the poor, often in part athletic prep schools for talented but academically weak athletes. With respect to discussion of these issues, college and university campuses provide more of an open forum than, say, a crossroads store in Missis-sippi. At the same time, civil rights and equality issues on campuses no longer excite great numbers of students or faculty.

Is this the best the university has to offer? Obviously not, and taking the university at its own best evaluation of itself, I would still ask that it become a more compassionate place, a more cooperative one, and a more honest one. More compassionate in recognizing how much suc-cess in the university is still the measure of success on the verge of adult life. Our suicides attributable to falling short in educating toward a career are fewer than those in Japan, but they are alarmingly high in prestige universities and among students studying for careers. Nor am I calling for a soft succoring of the relatively lame and halt. I am simply saying let mercy temper justice and let justice be broader than what academic grading and testing claims it to be. Compassion as I would have it would be some counter to mechanical bureaucratic functioning, some counter to the adoration of mind that stultifies feeling.

Perhaps more compassion would arise naturally if cooperation rather than competition more ruled the students' lives. Faculty should not be excluded either, for the jockeying for promotion and tenure has turned too many promising teachers into reluctant researchers or turned them out of the university altogether. Surely working with others has as much to recommend it as a way of learning as learning in solitude. Surely the rewards of doing things well together are as fulfilling to the many as the singular achievement is to the one.

Finally, compassion and cooperation would make honesty come easier, as respects the institution as well as individuals. If this poor be-nighted college, chronically in debt and forced to accept what faculty and students it can get on the open market, could but give up its compulsion to maintain the image of richly endowed and publicly supported institu-tions, could be honest about those limited things it can do both within and for the actual community surrounding it, would it not accomplish more of value than fudging and falling short? And if that mega-university could be honest about its relation between megabucks and megaton bombs, could be honest about its public show and private decay, would that not be a start toward regaining some of the character that should be at the heart of an institution of higher learning?

3

The Joys of Teaching

*C*haracter has its forbidding side. If it did not, human beings would probably develop it more easily than they commonly do. Character often seems composed chiefly of not doing what one wants to do, the patience to put up with what one should do, and the suffering of what life forces us to do. Adversity is said to be a prime builder of character; a certain grimness of demeanor, a gritting of teeth and tightness about the jaw may be a result.

Teaching has its need for duty and discipline and patience, if not downright suffering, but there is a joyful, spontaneous, and even ecstatic side of teaching that makes it immensely attractive. In this respect teaching is analogous to sex, the surface analogies pointing to deeper affinities seldom acknowledged within the institutional realities that shape a teacher's practice. The analogy may hold even here; some denial of joy seems to accompany the institutionalization of sex as well as of learning.

Teaching and Sex

Let us take up some of the obvious similarities and see where that leads. Consider, for example, how much anticipation is a part of the joy of teaching. The really good class is one for which the teacher prepares as joyfully and obsessively as a lover for a beloved. Consider how teaching at best, whether in the individual class or across a term, builds toward a climax, and arrives there with a sense of illumination that approximates physical consummation. Consider particularly how a really good class leaves a teacher physically exhausted, not perhaps ready to fall asleep but suffused with a satisfying kind of tiredness that, when the nerves quiet down, will bring dreamless sleep.

Socrates recognized all this. The *Symposium* is about teaching and learning as much as it is about love. Pregnancy as a metaphor for learning, and the split human selves, each half looking to join the other, are both brought forward in the *Symposium*. Moreover, there is Alcibiades, lusting for Socrates' body as he has lusted before, drawn to him as teacher as well as from physical passion — failed pupil in both respects, deserting Athenian responsibilities and selling out to the enemy despite Socrates' influence and tutelage, and unable to make it with Socrates besides. Yet, Socrates seems not to have given up on him in the *Symposium*; something good might yet be made of that brilliance of mind and passionate nature.

The sexual revolution has had its direct effect upon teaching as upon all aspects of modern life. During the sixties, traditional barriers between students and teachers broke down as they had never done before. As political involvement often provides the propinquity and common passion that invites sex, so, too, does teaching. More liaisons between students and teachers are a fact of recent campus life, though probably not as prevalent or as steamy as publicized news stories and campus novels imply. *Time* magazine's 1980 story, "Fighting Lechery on Campus," did not disclose much lechery: a suit filed at Yale, a charge against a Berkeley professor for "fondling and propositioning," kissing on the lips or forehead at Harvard, and a dismissal for sexual misconduct at San Jose State. A sociologist's survey (Skeen, 1981) of seven campuses in the Denver area resulted in interviews with eleven students and fourteen professors who had engaged in affairs. The prevailing pattern was a beginning in friendship and respect, a closeness in age — twenty-seven the median age of student, thirty-three of professor — and a likehood that affairs originated as much with female students as with male professors. Another observer (Taylor, 1981) notes that female graduate students and male professors have particular attractions for each other, such relationships sometimes ending in the professor's divorce and remarriage to the student.

A specific example of changing attitudes toward sexual relationships within academia arises out of the activities of the Danforth Foundation in support of higher education. The Danforth Associates program, begun in the 1930s, identified faculty members whose teaching was distinguished by their close relationships with students. The program provided the professors recognition and participation in conferences and small stipends for books and for entertaining students in their homes. By the seventies, home was no longer what it had been. The national meeting to which associates and their spouses were invited at foundation expense began to face such peculiar requests as the associate who wanted to "bring the one he loved" but who happened not to be his wife. A major speaker, invited to one conference, wanted to bring her lover, who happened to be of the same sex. "A significant other" became the language adopted to designate live-in relationships sanctified presumably by love but not by marriage.

Who would have thought in 1950 that a college of education, even in southern California, would have begat a "love professor?" Yet, by the mid seventies, Leo Buscaglia, professor of education at the University of Southern California, had played to more or less packed houses across the country. His books, *Love, Personhood*, and *Living, Loving & Learning*, get shuffled among Education, Inspiration, Psychology, and Human Sexuality at campus bookstores. Some of his success resides in the durable appeal of inspirational homilies: "Learn again to trust!" "Don't make love to a body, make love to a person." "Love is life in all of its aspects." "Are you truly the *you* of you?" But he is also read and listened to because he has not paralyzed his subject with academic solemnities. Beneath the manner is an engagement with the genuinely important relationships between love and teaching and learning.

Most of this kind of social change was good for teaching, for it forced recognition of how human and intensely personal teaching is likely to be. A heightened sense of the importance of personal relationships removed some barriers that kept students at too great a distance from professors. It helped keep institutions swollen by size and encumbered with regulations, less regular, more human, than they otherwise might have been. It helped to create more tolerance for a response to life that was not primarily cognitive and competitive. It also assisted in confronting, in the name of love, some of the barbarities of violence and war and technology. That it also often trivialized and debased love, dissolved both heart and mind in dope and dopey philosophy is not to be denied. Nor is it to be denied that among consenting adults, the personal and intense incline to sexual passion.

But I am not trying to strike a balance between the good and bad effects of the sexual revolution. The analogy between sex and teaching holds in repressive as well as permissive times. Sex and conversation, for example: Let's do it so we can talk, or conversely, let's talk ourselves into it. Yet, the greatest moment of communion between lovers is when the talking stops. This relationship between passion and thought and verbalizing, the progression from verbal stimulation to inner understanding to related action, are worth contemplating in teaching. We tend to talk too much as teachers, tend to think we are only doing our jobs when we are informing others by verbalizing what we know. We persist despite the fact that telling someone to do something does not get very high marks as a sure way of affecting the other person's actions. We should know this as parents, having demonstrated it so often as children to our own parents. As a formal system of communication, talk by itself does not even fix concepts or ideas very well, hence the emphasis teachers place on note taking or on the use of other means — diagrams, slides, demonstrations — to reinforce the verbal message. If there must be talk, dialogue draws the other person in, makes a student an active participant, increases the chance of retention and recall, and enhances the possibility of affecting action.

But what talking and sex also should remind us of is that much of talk is not to convey information. Talk may simply be the lovers' sweet nothings, surely as banal as the average classroom lecture, that establish the necessary relationship. The most important impact lecturing may have is not the transfer of information but, like the lovers' words, the stimulation to the act of learning. No wonder lecturing is in bad favor for both students and faculty. Both may want to make love — or learn — and one ends up talking the other to death.

Schwab (1978) has pursued all this with passion and intelligence in an essay titled "Eros and Education." "Eros," he writes, "the energy of wanting, is as much the energy source in the pursuit of truth as it is in the motion toward pleasure, friendship, fame, or power" (p. 109). He describes with precision the erotic elements by which a relationship is established between a teacher and class. It begins, as does love, in mutual needs — that of a member of a class to be recognized as an individual person; that of the teacher to be recognized as being needed. A relationship having been established, Schwab writes, the student will engage both in testing and in provocative, seductive behavior. "'Testing' behavior, then, is designed to estimate the teacher's Eros for the student, his charity. Impeding and provocative behavior test the teacher's strength. If any person is to put himself in some way into the hands of another, he must have assurance both of his gentleness and of his strength and competence" (p. 115). Not incidentally, Schwab's discussion of Eros arises and ends in a consideration of the precise merits and outcomes of discussion as a mode of teaching.

In the undergraduate college, ideally, the lecture should be conceived of as almost entirely designed to stimulate the student's desire to learn; through discussion a more vital, erotic, relationship can be established by which learning actually occurs. (The designation of *undergraduate college* is purposeful; in graduate school and often before, the classroom exchange between teacher and student often becomes as formalized and as deadly as routine sexual relationships in a long-suffered marriage.) Beginning with stimulation as a main objective, faculty might develop a sensitivity to the students' learning, rather than being preoccupied either with their own verbalizing or scholarship. Women understand this matter of talk and love better than men; that may account, in part, for women's greater receptivity to learning about teaching. As a sexual partner, it is the male who has the greatest difficulty in reaching the kind of communicating that the woman desires. Why? Perhaps because sex for the male is so much a pure physical release, an assertion of power, something apart from a communion of spirit that begins in talk and ends in silent rapture. So, the bad lecturer is not so much engaging some parts of the feeling and thinking apparatus of students as releasing his own stored-up knowledge and asserting the power that knowledge has given him.

To a teacher interested in pushing these conjectures further, I offer a series of questions:

How can I get that concentration, both over time and in its immediate intensity, that characterizes a physical passion? If any student, say, so had physics on his or her mind, verbalized over it, dwelt on it waking or sleeping, had moments of intensely embracing this and that vital theory, what vast learning might take place.

How can I change my students as love can and does change them, not in one particular accomplishment or mastery of some separate knowledge, but wholly?

How can I release the flow of words that comes with romantic seizure, my own words teasing and informing and valuing and caressing at the same time? And how can I match my words to the needs of the other, to both set example and free the other into making known what he may not have realized he knew?

How can I leave off verbalizing, conceptualizing, and yet not leave off learning? And how transmit that to students, to reinforce their own confidence without which learning goes poorly, to establish for them the feeling of growing, as Thoreau said, "like corn in the night?"

How can I, in short, as Socrates most of all did, work in full awareness that erotic love is both a metaphor for and an actuality of learning, that acting wisely in light of this knowledge is fundamental to arriving at some glimmer of the Socratic "good"?

If I would advocate one path to achieving teaching of the highest kind, I think I would choose the path of "loving" above any other. In a sense, all teachers subscribe to it, but many are inhibited in their practices. Only schoolgirls — our students — say things like "I *love* biology" or "I just *love* tennis," or even "I just *love* my professor." And yet most professors would not be professors if they did not love their subjects or their students or their daily work.

Loving One's Subject or Students or Work

Few professors, for example, would speak against loving one's subject. The "master" teachers Epstein (1981, p. xii) picks out in his somewhat Olympian view of great teachers all have in common "love of their subjects, an obvious satisfaction in arousing this love in their stu-

dents, and an ability to convince them that what they are being taught is
deadly serious." A manifest love of subject is often the key to the mystery
of how bad teachers can still affect some students greatly. Despite a cur-
mudgeonly manner or a lack of or wanton disregard for ordinary teaching skills, the professor conveys how deeply he is engaged in his subject
matter and, for some, what it is like to have and sustain that kind of love.

For many students, however, even a passionate love of subject
matter is not enough to offset the daily confusion or humiliation or
despair that a one-sided love affair customarily arouses. Then, too,
a great love for even a great subject matter may narrow rather than
broaden one's vision. Worse, it may create the gestures of defensiveness
and superiority that divide a university into enclaves of jealous lovers
protecting their beloved subjects. Love should bring generosity, the
expanded heart, but we know it often moves in a contrary way. Unre-
quited love — the failure to be recognized within the world that comprises
one's discipline — may have the worst kinds of effects, turning the teacher
into a cynic or misanthrope, morbidly loving that which gives him little
obvious return and openly hostile to all else. Finally, the purity of a love
of subject matter — the very way in which it displaces erotic passion —
may inhibit the expression of love in more personal ways that can affect
teaching positively in the interchange between learning individuals.

A love of subject matter can partially explain a seeming disdain
for or impatience with students. The trite split over teaching subjects
or students raises serious questions about the nature of objective truth,
the scholar's as against the teacher's primary responsibility, the security and insecurity of one human self confronting other selves, and the
nature of love to be both exclusive and inclusive. The freeing that went
on in the sixties has not resulted in a general easiness among professors about loving their students. It is dangerous; it is distracting; it is
improper; it is ridiculous; it is humanizing. And yet, we cannot flourish
as teachers without loving our students as we love our work.

Here we might better confront the mysteries of love than the techniques of teaching. For love can both tyrannize and free the beloved,
sequester lovers or place them admirably before the world, sympathize
and smother, energize and enfeeble, excuse cruelty and sanctify passion.
It is, as Greek thought clearly recognized, both monster and mistress:
Medea calling her children in to be murdered; Athena casting the decid-
ing vote for Orestes. Humanistic education needs no greater defense

than this: that more than any other aspect of education, it has pondered the mysteries of the deepest of human relations and shed that light which the experiences and writings of men and women through the centuries has cast. How much there is in a single sonnet of Shakespeare's — in, for example, Sonnet 129, which begins:

> Th' expense of spirit in a waste of shame
> Is lust in action; and till action, lust
> Is perjur'd, murd'rous, bloody, full of blame,
> Savage, extreme, rude, cruel, not to trust.

Though the humanities still lay claim to such witnesses as Shakespeare, the academic scrutiny of love has passed over largely to the behavioral sciences. Courses in human sexuality have flourished, incorporating both what can be diagrammed and photographed — here is the male organ, there the female — with inquiry into inner states of being and social behavior. The most titillating campus news of 1982 was about the tenured professor at Long Beach State (Dolar, 1982) whose teaching of the Psychology of Sex allegedly included optional homework in new sexual activity such as group, extramarital, homosexual, and casual sex. A newspaper interview in which he had admitted becoming "romantically involved" with three or four students precipitated his suspension by the university and subsequently his resignation. In a statement distributed to his colleagues, he wrote, "While I admit to some minor misjudgments, on the whole I feel very comfortable with my role in the matter."

Such an incident, uncommon in actuality if not in fantasy and folklore, can contribute to considerations of a teacher's love of subject as related to love of students. Here an attachment to a specific subject matter may have seemed to legitimize a romantic attachment to students. But quite outside acquiring expertise in the behavioral sciences, a teacher might be expected to have pondered more carefully the essentially erotic relationship that can exist between teacher and student, subject matter aside. Ionesco's *The Lesson*, for example, is probably as instructive as any pedagogic text. The professor in this short play who is coaching his female pupils to the Doctorates and Super Doctorates is also killing and burying them, one by one, to the count of forty as the play ends. The way in which Ionesco shows sexless pontificating giving way to undisguised lust is marvelous, not just because of his comic brilliance but also because he exposes one of the fundamental realities of teaching and learning. Knowledge *is* power, and power demands possession, and sexual possession is the male's driving urge. The professor in the play does not possess his pupils, though his lust becomes menacingly obvious and their own sexuality manifest as the play proceeds. Ultimately, he kills them, driven to a frenzy, ostensibly by their failure to learn, but more by their failure to yield to his own learning.

The sexual freedoms of our time and the clinical regard for sexuality in academe are both contributors to misunderstandings about the love that exists between student and teacher. Private relations that are "intimate" and "personal" become "public" and "depersonalized." Given the scientific analogies by which professing is governed, the presence of controlled experiments in sexuality as part of classroom practices—within an appropriate discipline—is more surprising by its infrequency than by the occasional publicized incident. On that analogy, English departments long ago established writing clinics to take care of fractured syntax and prose fevers. Given, also, the split between mind and body, which Greek and Christian thought established and Descartes wed to modern science, an unwise professor honoring that split as truth can easily set aside moral injunctions that would regulate physical behavior. Manipulations of the body are but one more instance of the inexorable logic of matter.

My own argument is that the love that arises between teacher and pupil must retain a respect for the sacredness of person, a recognition that more than the pineal gland connects spirit and substance. Both Greek and Christian thought are wise in these recognitions. They should be, for they have observed them for centuries and arrived at attitudes and precepts that offer some guidance for our culture today. The love between student and teacher is precious and special just as it stops short of possession, not just because of cultural sanctions or institutional regulations but because of its own inner nature. Recent scientific investigations of incest have not yet overturned the ordinary perception that fathers and mothers do not customarily and without adverse consequences violate their children. From these premises, I argue here that discovery of how one serves learning by a love engendered between student and teacher is a study deserving one's highest respect and wisdom.

What I have been saying with some intensity about love of subject and love of student can be said more dispassionately about love of work.

Work is, for the most part, dispassionate. It is, for the majority of human beings, what we have to do in order to do some of what we want. Professors do and should recognize how favored they are by having enjoyable work that is motivated more by inner than outer compulsions. Though some professors do give up positions for attractions of other careers, few repudiate academic careers over dissatisfaction with the work. Across the professoriate and among the various responsibilities that constitute academic work, teaching arouses the highest degree of satisfaction and this despite the high values institutions place on research.

Teaching and Joy

Csikszentmihalyi (1975) has devoted a book to describing the most intense kind of experience that arises from learning. It is essentially a description of joy, of the kind of free play Thoreau (1973 [1854], pp. 316–317) describes of a hawk in spring:

> . . . alternately soaring like a ripple and tumbling a rod or two over and over, showing the underside of its wings, which gleamed like a satin ribbon in the sun, or like the pearly inside of a shell. . . . It was the most ethereal flight I had ever witnessed. It did not simply flutter like a butterfly, nor soar like the larger hawks, but it sported with proud reliance in the fields of air; mounting again and again with its strange chuckle, it repeated its free and beautiful fall, turning over and over like a kite, and then recovering from its lofty tumbling, as if it had never set its foot on *terra firma*. It appeared to have no companion in the universe—sporting there alone—and to need none but the morning and the ether with which it played. It was not lonely, but made all the earth lonely beneath it.

Csikszentmihalyi calls this kind of ecstatic condition "flow" experience and exhorts teachers to elicit such a response from students for whom learning is more often fraught with boredom and anxiety. He does not choose the university lecture platform and classroom to illustrate "flow" but turns to learning in which the physical and mental conjoin: rock climbing, for example, which to most would seem an unlikely place to explore collegiate learning. Yet the connection is not as unlikely as it might seem.

Long before rock climbing developed the techniques that now

distinguish it as a sport, mountain climbing attracted great numbers of highly articulate men and women. Many were British dons or American professors, in part because professing gave them free time in summers and a sedentary vocation may have impelled them to physical activity. Perhaps it is more than that: mountains have a physical immensity not unlike the immensity of knowledge. For scholars, there are always higher peaks, abstract vistas drawing them on. Moreover, mountain climbing has the simplicity of the concrete over the abstract. There *is* a highest mountain in this world and it can be, has now been, climbed. The dweller in the abstraction of knowledge only has peaks and valleys, hidden couloirs, new ranges opening up from whatever perspective one attains, and now and again a supremely high peak someone climbs. It may be that the rock climber has given up mountaineering's grand adventuring and sense of conquest for a more at-hand experiencing. And yet in that terribly constricted experience, that slow-motion partnership between mind and body, that risking within carefully controlled limits of safety, is an experience of learning that stands for some totality of life's experience.

Csikszentmihalyi (1975) describes flow experience as characterized above all by a deep, spontaneous involvement with the task at hand. In flow, one is so carried away by interaction as to feel immersed in the activity; the distinction between "I" and "it" becomes irrelevant. "Attention is focused on whatever needs to be done, and there is not enough left over to worry or get bored or distracted" (p. 9). We are, to be sure, idealizing here, about rock climbing as about any other learning. There are days when one cannot get into the rhythm that is so much a part of flow, when the hands neither move nor fingers grip nor legs hold as they should. But, to those who continue on in this exercise of mind and body, flow does happen on the best of days and brings one back to learn more.

College learning, as Csikszentmihalyi (1982) and others have pointed out, is too little attended with flow experience. Many students probably never experience it. Some few experience it fully, and probably because they have been brought to the mountains, so to speak, by the right teacher and led to experience what he or she has experienced and in the same way. I can still remember how some five years after first being exposed to Greek and after a period of solitary study, I knew enough of the structure of that language to feel as if it were there below me; a hitherto cluttered landscape had resolved itself into a marvelous design, which could now be perceived from the height I had reached. I had arrived there by much drudgery. I have long since descended; lost what close acquaintance with Greek I then had. But for the moment that feeling was sure, a promise that other drudgery might lead to other rewards. Most important of all was that a teacher had brought me to the mountain, had endowed long-term study with an ultimate value, had stood surety for a flow experience that would only come after much hard scrambling.

A humanities professor, Nancy Hill (1980, p. 48), developed the analogy between the teacher and the mountaineer in an essay for the *Chronicle of Higher Education*. "The teacher as mountaineer," she writes, "learns to connect. The guide rope links mountain climbers together so that they may assist one another in the ascent. The teacher makes a 'rope' by using the oral and written contributions of the students, by forging interdisciplinary and intradisciplinary links where plausible, and by connecting the course material with the lives of the students where possible and with the wider national life where pertinent. . . . The teacher is not a pleader, not a performer, not a huckster, but a confident, exuberant guide on expeditions of shared responsibility into the most exciting and least-understood terrain on earth — the mind itself."

But enjoyable as the majority of college teachers find their work, all have to face some split between the fun and games of college going and the drudgery of academic work. The paradox of all formal education is that it takes an essentially pleasurable and natural inclination and turns it into an at times grim and enforced activity. It stretches, by law, through childhood and adolescence and by social pressures even beyond that. In moving from the lower schools to higher education, the teachers' preoccupation with physical discipline gives way to another kind of grimness: an emphasis upon academic rigor befitting the importance of one's studies and the consequences of failure. You must, our institutions say, keep up your grade-point average else you won't get into medical school or a good graduate school or even get past the freshman year. We must, our tough-minded faculty say, hold our students to high standards else our bridges will fall, our elevators jam, our nuclear devices explode in their silos. Perhaps so, but our grim pursuit of grim things has in many respects made it difficult for our common humanity to shore us up, to keep our violent impulses from blowing us apart. Maybe, like Christian martyrs of old, we should at least go singing to the lions.

We have other choices than either being scientifically impeccable or Christian martyrs. We might rate joy in our work higher than we do and as institutions seem to allow. The most conspicuous example of the paradox of grimness and joy in higher learning is how American academic institutions in this century have made public spectacles of the joys of youth (no more intensely felt than by aging alumni) even as they have countenanced a lack of excitement, a dutiful carrying out of chores, a protracted game of winners and losers in academic work. At worst, the academic program is preparation for a life in which the mind operates as it must in order to afford vicarious pleasures for the body. "The heavy bear," as Delmore Schwartz (1938) called our physical selves, is fastened to us not only by our biological natures but by our thinking selves who may be creating much of that heaviness. The actual bear leads an existence dominated by an endless foraging for existence; the metaphorical bear is an ingratiating figure in its living landscape, an idler, provocateur, games player who can learn to dance.

The wedding of abstract concepts to the world itself, of books to mountains, of learning stored in the mind to that felt in the gut, is a high goal to set before almost any class. A step toward that goal is one that leaves behind the common suspicions that students always seek the easy path, cannot be brought to learning, have been spoiled by the feebleness of past education, and are intractable beyond the promise of immediate rewards and threat of punishment. Take them for what they are, much the same as what we are, or were, and excite the mutual joy of moving even one step along the way of "Now I know. See, I have learned!"

A troubled teacher at one of the seminars I have conducted on teaching asked the question: "Here I've had what seemed to me a really good class. The students were attentive and responsive. We genuinely exchanged ideas and raised questions. Many seemed to be having a good time and so did I. Afterwards a number came up and thanked me for a class that was really fun. But my question is, did they learn anything? Was I just entertaining? How can I tell when I've had a really good class, one in which students really learned?"

Only an exaggerated respect for boredom, pain, and fear as indexes of learning could bring on such extreme doubts. There is some circumstantial evidence, like finding a trout in the milk, Thoreau said, that is very convincing. The outward physical signs that denote a receptive inner state are good indications of learning. Clearly, there is nothing more fundamental to learning than giving attention to the task. Attention registers in as obvious physical ways as smiles and laughter. If, in the end, a range of attentive responses results in students actually saying they were pleased, why should we distrust their response, fear they are conning us or deceiving themselves about easy pleasures as against hard learning? We should not, for the basic enjoyment in any experience is the satisfaction of wants. In the classroom, surely one underlying want is to learn, even though the mutual cant of teachers and students is to assume that any displays of satisfaction have to do with some lesser parts of the student's functioning self.

Trust and the Pleasures of Learning

Teaching arouses a great deal of self-doubt, but it necessarily demands large amounts of self-trust. Self-doubt and self-trust are closely related to the amount of doubt and trust a teacher holds toward his or her students. My own philosophic stance is that however skeptical we may be at times, we must, over the long run, be ruled more by trust in ourselves and in our students.

I have never satisfactorily resolved the conflict that college teachers commonly set up between teaching and entertaining. The reverse side is the positive attraction many college teachers find in boredom. I think it has to do, once again, with the split between mind and body. The mind needs little of the physical titillations associated with entertainment; the body can be instantly pleased, easily diverted, often by gross things. The mind has purity; the body would feed on swill. Our whole tendency to value abstractions places physical responses in a lesser light.

And yet, college professors are not notable for eschewing pleasure. The world in which they work offers them a wider variety of entertainment than most other milieus and less of a separation between what one does for work and for fun. Music, theater, sports are close at hand, not confined to the formal occasion, though it should be acknowledged that faculty members busy at their important tasks are unlikely to stop in at the art gallery or music hall during the working day. Some sense of guilt may be aroused from working in a pleasant environment. Doing tasks that are satisfying, congenial, even pleasurable may provoke a reflex gesture that teaching must not be conspicuously entertaining.

The metaphor of sex may add something to these speculations. Surely, the sexual act is one of the most intensely pleasurable of acts, yet one, if we go by the degree of sexual maladjustment that seems to be in our society, attended by much self-doubt and little self-trust. If one has to ask, after it is over, whether it really was pleasurable, whether it really did connect to some vital and pure part of both partners' wanting, if one has to ponder whether he or she is a good lover, something less than a satisfactory sex life may be implied. If we cannot as teachers perceive in shared joy some incitement to learning, some evidence, circumstantial to be sure, that learning is going on, then we rob ourselves of the joy that should be in our work, a circumstantial evidence, in itself, of a shared love of subject and others and ourselves.

Teaching and Sexism

One final and important matter falls within the subject we are pursuing. The feminist movement has called into question most of our assumptions about relationships between sexes. It has also disclosed the extent and kind of sexual discrimination against women faculty members and the wider social impact of such discrimination.

The salient facts are well established. The basic conditions persist despite a decade of pressure and legislation to improve them: women faculty earn less than men, occupy more of part-time, lower-rank, and nontenured positions, hold fewer administrative positions, are found in greater numbers in departments identified with women (for example, nursing and home economics) and in fewest numbers in those identified with men (for example, the hard sciences). Sadly, the degree of discrimination roughly correlates with the prestige level of the college and university.

Much of this discrimination can be blamed upon regarding women as sex objects before marriage and begetters and raisers of children after. The very discussion I am conducting here has a masculine bias, if only because, like the overwhelming majority of college teachers, I am a male. Hence, this discussion of sexuality between teachers and students implies that the teacher is male, the student female, even though such is not my intent. More to the point is that a consideration of sexuality and teaching raises the central question that has been raised by the women's movement: overt discrimination aside, what are the effects upon a woman educated in institutions dominated by males?

The effects are obviously adverse, if one places value upon wide freedom of choice, acknowledges that competence is equally distributed among sexes, and gives up notions about a woman's proper place. As respects teaching as a career, nothing should stand in the way of recognition and achievement for women in any academic discipline.

The actualities are different and they arise not only from overt discrimination—the various ways dominant male faculty members have of keeping women in in their place—but also from faculty and student behavior hard to recognize or deal with. They are as obvious as the difficulties women students face in working in fields dominated by male faculty, and as subtle as the differences in the way faculty members—male and female—treat male and female students.

The Association of American Colleges' Project on the Status and Education of Women has recently published a detailed and documented study, "The Classroom Climate: A Chilly One for Women?" (Hall and Sandler, 1982). Its concern is with how, overtly and inadvertently, classroom teachers treat men and women differently and most often with adverse effects on women's learning. Behaviors that erode the confidence of women students are numerous and varied. Disparaging comments on women's intellectual abilities or specific capacities, sexist humor, condescending and patronizing replies to women's questions, questioning women's seriousness of purpose or choice of careers, comments about women's physical appearance or attributes, calling on male students more than female ones, suspicions toward older women or part-time students are only a few of these behaviors. In the more marked "male" climate of graduate and professional schools, such behaviors are likely to be more conspicuous. The damage to women graduate students, who already show a lesser degree of self-esteem than their male classmates, can not help but be consequential.

In the imbalances between numbers of men and women faculty in most disciplines, it is impossible to avoid having some departments take on macho characteristics. Engineering colleges and departments are closer to "man's work," the bloody work of war, for example, than are those in fine arts and humanities. They are characterized more by political conservatism. And though they may make much of the few women students they attract, they are bastions of male supremacy. To some degree, these propensities can be challenged, if not greatly affected, by legal and social pressures. Women faculty members can bring suit and some men faculty members go to jail to protect their masculine-arrived-at right to vote secretly against a woman if they choose. Such pressures have opened tightly closed doors at least a crack. As respects students, pressures against sexual discrimination have had at least the one curious effect of opening opportunities within the least academic of college enterprises — intercollegiate athletics. Despite the obvious equity in increasing dramatically this form of scholarship aid for women, it has been bought at the price of being brought into a carefully defined and controlled masculine enterprise. Their collective success is by that same old *manly* route that has always been open to women achievers. The ranks of those women who succeed as college teachers because they "think and produce like a man" have been swelled by those who can "run and shoot and pass like a man." At worst, this form of equity consists of spreading athletic corruption equally among the sexes.

A more sensitive recognition of equity for women might come from embracing the basic democratic premise: the recognition and acceptance of both equality and difference. We are still in a confused time when the press for equality between sexes denies the differences between them. Both sexual experiences and teaching can reward the sensitive participant, male and female, who examines what distinctive quality the other brings to these loving relationships. That does not mean accepting sexual stereotypes, nor does it deny the possessing and developing of qualities in either sex that may seem to be the more natural inclination of the other.

In a dozen years of speaking to hundreds of faculty groups assembled to discuss teaching, I have been struck by the fact that women faculty attend in greater numbers in proportion to their numbers on the faculty than men. Less confidently, I would say that these women faculty often show a more intense interest in teaching and a greater responsiveness to its widest dimensions than men. A number of surveys have given evidence that women value teaching as a main source of satisfaction more than men. All of these may be explained in terms of the conditioning within teaching that women have experienced: they have been allowed to succeed at teaching, are forced into doing it, while men do more prestigious research. Still, I think it has much to do with the nature of teaching and learning and of women and men. A sexual relationship begins in differences and ends in harmony. One gives and one receives, yet both are givers and receivers, aggressors and defenders, active and passive.

That is part of the most vital lesson teachers must learn. And it is a lesson best taught when there is enough balance — in numbers and prestige and recognition and confidence — between men and women faculty members to make interchange possible. The difference was observed by the male president of Brown University, William Herbert Perry Faunce (1916): "When womanhood with its swift intuition, its wealth of sympathy, its strong personal conviction, its assertion of the soul, enters the realm of scholarship, it ought to sweep before it all learned pettifogging as the morning sun scatters the clinging mists. It should irradiate knowledge with the light of wisdom, and should visualize it with a great human purpose."

Lest we smile at the quaintness of Faunce's rhetoric, such public statements were part of the necessary assailing of masculine sensibilities that led to women's suffrage not long after this was written. The glorious day he envisions is still far away. Learned pettifogging resists the combined efforts of both male and female. Irradiating knowledge with the light of wisdom may, like the perfect uniting of spirit and body, be more realized in the ideal than the actual. Nevertheless, the ideals of teaching can be well served by enlarging the possibilities for women to assert some parity of "feminine" characteristics, if you will, against the prevailing masculine ones. The argument for true female-male equality in higher education is as simple as that given by Dean Robert Pollack (Katz, 1982, p. 20) when asked why he welcomed Columbia's change into a coed college: "Because half of the smart people in the country are women."

Strong voices continue to be heard from women who refuse to exist in what Carolyn Heilbrun (1976, p. 32) describes as "an irreversible state of fear in the presence of their male colleagues." Women, she reminds male administrators, comprise very large numbers of undergraduate and graduate students. Such students "must learn their own political and economic power, and stop acting like charity children at a Christmas party." The poet and professor Adrienne Rich (1975, p. 32) envisions "a woman-centered university" different from the present hierarchal man-centered ones that use women as means to accomplish male work. "Within and without academe," she writes, "the rise in women's expectations has gone far beyond the middle class and has released an incalculable new energy — not merely for changing institutions but for human redefinition; not merely for equal rights but for a new kind of being."

4

Craft, Science, or Art?

*T*he remarks college faculty members make reveal an odd regard
for teaching. In my own work, I often face faculty members who are curious about both how and why a professor of English would involve himself in such an activity as improving teaching. The "how" questions are
asked by faculty members working against the grain to raise the attention given to teaching on a local campus. Some would like to widen the
scope of their own activities or take heart from sharing their interests
with an outsider. The "why" questions sometimes show a suspicion of
motives, and some seem to seek peculiar reasons that will explain why an
English teacher does not stick to his disciplinary subject. Has he failed as
a scholar? Been somehow drummed out of his discipline? Others accept
the motivation as arising from strong and respectable convictions about
teaching, but wonder if it is possible to maintain one's standing in the
discipline and still do this kind of thing. At the extreme are barely polite
questions that attack the presumption of any one professor trying to tell

other professors how to teach. In a number of instances, questioners have expressed polite surprise that this visitor's presentation suggested he might be a good teacher. It was as if a visiting scholar talking about teaching should not teach at all or teach poorly, or that if this visitor showed some signs of teaching well, that possibility should not be publicly disclosed.

Most professors teach, but many may not regard teaching as their principal vocation. Donors and taxpayers pay professors to teach, yet recognize that much else beside teaching is supported by colleges and universities. Teaching is clearly no one thing, an identifiable art or science or pedagogic subject. It relates to all subject matters and is still outside most of these subject matters. In writing a previous book about teaching, I chose to call teaching a "craft" and was surprised to find faculty members asking why I chose that term. Like students who, with the right questions, often demonstrate more knowing than they think they possess, I seemed to have many reasons for regarding teaching as a craft.

Craft as Guile

First of all, craft is associated with slyness: crafty as a fox. Who is to deny that foxes are good teachers of chickens and owners of henhouses? A teacher's effectiveness, if we would but admit it, is composed of the tricks of the trade, devices used spontaneously and regularly to attract and hold attention, or specific devices connected with helping students master particular concepts or skills. One such device is that skill of questioning by which a student's learning is drawn out or *educed*, as the word *educate* still incorporates. These bags of tricks are the magician's tricks by which a good sleight-of-hand artist can hold a crowd enthralled, exciting some to rush home to try their own tricks. Surely that is an essential of teaching, whether we call it art or craft: to enthrall if we are able, or at least to gain and hold the learner's attention. After we have gained that attention, then the trick is to provoke the learner to practice the acquiring of a skill or to search out the answers to questions or to imitate the acts of mind and muscle that have been set forth.

Craft is not entirely guile, and therefore its usage may escape the adverse connotations attached to trickery and deception. Anyone who has watched or worked with a skilled craftsman recognizes the kinds of tricks and devices I am talking about. They are not created for effect or even economy of effort but have as an end the best way of arriving at a finished product that will be both useful and esthetically pleasing. They may be as small as the way in which a master woodworker brings a tool to a razor-sharp edge with a few strokes of a whetstone. Or they may be the more complex acts of selecting and cutting and bringing out the grain in a piece of wood as if the worker has seen inside to affirm it was there. The secrets of a craft are those accumulations of trial and error, lucky coincidence, momentary insights, and long purposeful seeking that become practices, the way a job gets done. Observant teachers working with human materials learn in the same way; their secrets are their combination of simple practices that work to complex ends.

College teachers probably have too quick a reaction to gimmicks, just as they have an unwise propensity to oppose "entertainment" to "learning." As in any craft, there are good and bad gimmicks, a fine line between being tricky and tricksy. On the one hand, elocutionary devices learned by the book and performed by rote are likely to be mere trickery. On the other hand, even such an outrageous device as that of an economics professor who ostensibly permitted students to pay for their grades may be both arresting and highly instructional.

I have in mind, in the first instance, an English professor who intruded into a talk about Shakespeare's life an anecdote about some female member of an English court who, in some century, put out the eyes of tame pigeons with her knitting needle. The story may have been loosely intended to illustrate the manners of a past age, but its chief purpose was in the telling of it. When the pigeon had been blinded, the lady, so this lecturer said, would clap her little hands and put the bird blindly in flight. "Like this," he said, clapping his hands, and asking his audience to clap their hands too. The anecdote brought the audience to attention by the gratuitous cruelty of the story and by the forced physical response, but I cannot imagine that such an elocutionary device did much to establish anything about the subject at hand. In the other instance, the professor's strategy, which had greatly to do with emphasizing the underlying economic motive for most human acts, had to be convincing enough to bring students to the point of playing for real and yet stop short of actually going through with such unethical behavior.

Deliberate deceit may be ill chosen or well chosen, poorly or deftly executed, and effective as both choice and execution raise the level of learning of a greater number of students. Three principles seem to underlie the use of almost any device: the device must be closely and accurately related to the skill or principle of subject matter under study; it must not place the students in prolonged and actual jeopardy about their behavior; and it must be resolved in a way that furnishes a greater illumination or motivation than would be possible by other means. The study of nuclear physics surely owes a great debt to the inventor of the mousetraps and ping-pong balls that illustrated a nuclear reaction even though atoms may not be anything like ping-pong balls.

Being crafty on the teacher's part may mean always staying one jump ahead of the students. On the student's part, it may mean the establishment of a necessary independence from even the most persuasive of teachers. Watching several cycles of students over thirty years, I find most disturbing those who have been with us since the mid seventies who, perhaps in reaction to the questioning sixties, want only to be told what they should learn and how and even to what end. The crafty teacher will not let students be simply passive sponges, but will fool, deceive, trick, all in the interest of getting students to question, to find out for themselves, to respond to the complexity of the world and to nature's proclivity for hiding and deceiving.

Craft, as used here, may seem intentionally to be associated with games and play. Learning is often the highest form of play, the best game around. To put it another way, the learning that takes place in games, or which young people undertake on their own to be able to play games well, outstrips most of what goes on in a college classroom. If we would develop our craft, we classroom teachers must recognize that we compete with other learning that may afford more gratification than does ours. Much of what we teach can approach the condition of being highly attractive play without detracting from its import. If we cannot be playful at all in teaching, we are probably ill suited for that vocation.

Craft and Humility

The word *craft* as applied to teaching can be usefully associated with craft in woodworking and pottery and quiltmaking. I like the humility that resides in craftwork, and which does not keep men and women who practice crafts from developing great excellence. The democratic associations of crafts are appropriate for American education, for it has long aimed at affecting the broad expanse of human potentiality rather than at catering to the select few. Craft demands attention to humble details and often entails working with everyday instruments and ordinary materials. Craft remains "handcraft" as contrasted with "machine made." The term thus offers some resistance to the tendency to regard machine technology as the panacea for instruction, to make instruction "teacher proof," as the jargon goes. Teaching is as much threatened as enhanced by an infatuation with equipment, these days often both complex and expensive. Even effective technology creates a distance between teacher and student not unlike that between workers on an industrial assembly line and their work. Teachers need the craftsman's intimate and caring and personal attention to his or her materials.

In using the word *craft*, I may seem to be too much emphasizing humble, even secondary skills, as compared with those that distinguish *art*. What a superb craftsman may achieve over a lifetime of applying craft may well be art, and few artists are not also superb craftsmen. Yet, common usage distinguishes between the two terms, and it is this distinction I am trying to clarify as regards teaching. I will say more about teaching as an art or science later in this chapter.

Craft and Utility

Craft is akin to the German *Kraft*, meaning power or strength. In our time of career-oriented education, no one needs reminding that students connect getting an education with getting a job, with acquiring a strength and power that makes it possible for them to perform well in society. There is nothing ignoble in that end, nor need its emphasis set up a conflict between liberal and vocational education. Liberal education, perceived as craft, confers its kind of strength and power, that of being able to function as a human being, parent, and citizen. Nor should such liberal education be assumed to be only a dealing with lofty abstractions. There is as much doing in being a good parent or a good citizen as in being a good plumber.

One of a handful of letters I have received from students sheds some light on the mixture of the practical and the ideal, craft and art, in teaching. It came from Hamburg, Germany, and reads as follows:

Dr. Eble,

I am (as you no doubt gathered from the return address) Dee Woolley. I was a student of yours fall '75. I am now serving a mission in North Germany, and have been doing so for a year now.

Today, I told my companion, who had asked me how to spell "ceiling," that I don't make the "except after 'c'" mistake any more, since a professor of mine circled the 'ie' it received in a paper of mine. You are he.

Naturally that isn't why I am writing this letter. You were one of the few (and only) teachers who gave me the low grades I deserved. Especially as I attempt to work up the German language into a usable tool, I see the value of working from the first, of using the gifts I have to learn, not to get by after not having done so.

Last night I noticed the sunset. The flatness of the plain around Hamburg makes the sunset much farther away than it used to be in Zion. It gave me opportunity to pause and think about the increased awareness I am feeling in so many areas.

Though the purpose of this letter and my source of motivation are still quite unclear to me, I must close.

I respect you greatly, and hope to attain some of the positive aspects I saw in you.

Sincerely,

Dee Woolley

I cite this letter not to parade "those positive aspects" someone saw in me, nor I hasten to add, to champion the virtues of exercising rigor in teaching and giving low grades. The grade I gave Mr. Woolley was not that low — it was a "C" — and I would rather err on the side of being too generous, too encouraging, with students than to delude myself by equating good teaching with how tough I can be. What most affects me about this letter is the writer's announced uncertainty as to why he was writing at all. It was, in part, and I take him at his word, to thank me for teaching him something useful. And it was, in another part, that I had opened him up to some values in learning that are hard to express because they are not attached to subject matters or skills but are nevertheless there and are important. Somehow, at least in this one instance, I have come up to Thoreau's advice: "Rescue the drowning and tie your shoestrings."

Learning One's Craft

Craft is a useful way of talking about how people learn to teach. Teaching is largely experientially acquired, grows by the doing of it, prospers by example and imitation. Thus, the best teacher training—a barbarous term, for training is what we give disobedient dogs and show horses—may be that of master and apprentice. By that means, too, we might be able to bring both master and apprentice to examine carefully and set forth clearly just what constitutes their skill. It is baffling that so many teachers are reluctant to articulate just what it is they do. Perhaps it is from a becoming modesty, or from a respect for the mysteries of teaching which analysis can threaten, or even from an unacknowledged disrespect that regards teaching skill as a secondary accomplishment not exact enough to be a science or sufficiently inspired to be an art.

In my book on the craft of teaching, much of the advice is of the kind one might get from reading up on a craft: in lecturing, for example, allow the audience time to settle in, establish and maintain eye contact, vary dynamics and tone of voice, break up large bodies of material into short segments, fashion beginnings and ends. McKeachie's *Teaching Tips* (1969) has had numerous reprintings because it does just that common-sense job—offers tips. A recent work coming out of the Harvard-Danforth Center for Teaching and Learning, *The Art and Craft of Teaching* (Gullette, 1982), is another example of a useful "how-to" book.

Much about any craft can be learned from books, but few craftsmen become expert by the book alone. Even such a simple thing as hitting a nail cannot be learned well without hitting a lot of nails. A smart amateur saves nails and thumbs by giving attention to how a skilled carpenter wields a hammer or perhaps by being shown by one that this is the way to do it.

Many of the particulars of teaching are as simple, complex, and identifiable as the many craft skills that develop best through experience and apprenticing. Some skills—like how to tell a good story—we pick up because we have been exposed to good story tellers and have been encouraged to tell our own. But even such a common skill as this is not possessed by everyone, may not have developed in a teacher by a natural and easy route.

One spring, a young teacher came to me in distress about how his teaching was going and asked me to visit his classes and give some help. I sat through two classes in which he appeared to be thoroughly in command of his subject and intensely concerned with getting that day's lesson across. But both classes went poorly. It seemed clear to me that he was trying to do too much, was too intense, and his students were like sprinters held for fifty minutes poised in the blocks. My main piece of advice was to relax, and as to particulars, I suggested he might here and there tell a joke. A year later, he invited me back to visit a class. He had relaxed, he said, had cut some things from his classes, and had had a good year. It was a better class by far by my measure, and there were the jokes, awkwardly told, and each almost visibly prefaced by "This is a joke." They were good jokes, however, brief anecdotes related closely to his subject, linguistics, and both funny and illuminating. I complimented him on a class that seemed to go very well. He thanked me and said, "Yes, and next year I'm going to learn to tell jokes really well."

Craft and Character

Many aspects of craft go beyond the manifestation of hand skills by which one arrives at serviceable and handsome objects. Here, I refer back to the shaping of character in which teachers have a part. A few years ago I visited a flea market outside Atlanta, Georgia. My attention centered on a bellows, not a very good one, insofar as the leather was cracked and as much air came out of the sides as from the nozzle. But as I was looking at it, the proprietor came over and said: "See the worn in it." Now that's folk talk, *Suthren* talk, what one might get from a craftsman whose act of language, like his act of hand, had a strong sense of use and practicality about it. But what I noticed too, and did not have the proper English words to express my admiration for, was "the worn" in it, the gray silver of the handles made by the hands of dozens of people over dozens of years pressing those handles and so breathing life into a fire that warmed some human hearth. In my sense of teaching, it is that sense of "the worn" that I most prize, what remains in students accumulated over the years and from dozens of minds and presences, and to which I have made some contribution. If I do my craft well, there is some chance that I will be part of "the worn" in students I have met.

Craft and Honesty

While I am pondering the words of common speech, why do we say "an honest craftsman?" I do not know how the expression arose; perhaps we link the words because it is hard to fake craft. Tables will totter and doors not close and the stuffing come out of comforters. Honesty is enforced by the presence of a user and by the measure of how a thing actually works. The merely decorative and the elaborations by which charlatans disguise their work are not present in the well-turned craft. Although I make no strong argument that craftsmen are honest by virtue of their craft, I find the possibility useful in regarding a teacher's practice. For surely, teachers should be honest about what they know and what they are trying to do and, above all, about their own ignorance.

College students faced with the tangible signs of great learning evoked, for example, by the library offices or laboratories in which their professors work, are likely to be impressed, if not cowed. "Have you read all those books?" students ask, looking at the bookshelves in my own office and not realizing that at no period in my thirty years of buying books (and getting desk copies free) could I have said "Yes" honestly. The same kind of perception is often shown to the professor's display of learning, facts on the tip of the tongue, problem solutions at the finger tips. Despairing of ever remembering so much, thinking so logically, students need be honestly and frequently told of what a shelf full of books and a quick study fifteen minutes before class can do. Or reminded that through repeated exposure to the same material over a great number of years some array of facts must stick, some habits of thought become deeply ingrained.

Because it is easy for students to despair of learning anything, faced as they are with so many who have presumably learned so much, I take some satisfaction that advanced age permits me to be more honest about my ignorance as about most aspects of teaching. I am more careful, more honest, about what we may "know" in any exact sense, about many of the subjects I teach. And more honest, too, about what knowing has to do with how we act and about how often we act without knowing much or in disregard of what we know. As a young teacher, I was often acutely embarrassed at being caught up in some mistaken assertion that I had been trapped into defending. Or I would find myself defending a grade or an assignment or a teaching practice in terms that would never stand up in court. Words are so easy to manipulate; as verbal manipulators, we teachers may have more day-by-day affinities with sellers of used cars and herbal essences than with builders of cabinets. So the image of an honest craftsman may be useful to maintain against temptations to be otherwise.

Is Teaching a Science?

I have been anecdotal and personal in discussing craft because I think teaching skills are acquired through personal development, observation and imitation, and shared experience. As a good mechanic is likely to develop by being thrown among a group of garrulous and skilled and experienced mechanics, so might good teachers develop within a group of professors good at and demonstrative about teaching.

My reflections on craft in teaching do not presume to establish the true nature of either. What about teaching as science and art? Some teachers make much of the science in teaching as others seriously regard it as an art. Though I welcome any attitudes that enhance teaching, I have some reservations about linking teaching too tightly to science and some fewer reservations about its relation to art.

Why not a science? The first objection arises out of a larger objection to using the word *science* to apply to all relatively precise and objective inquiry, particularly to those systematic inquiries characterized by the concerns and methods of the physical sciences. As argued in earlier chapters, the self, the person, matters of style and character and of human relationships are integral to teaching. The objectivity, replicability, uniformity of science are in crucial ways at odds with the personal, the improvisational, the idiosyncratic that distinguish teaching. To be sure, *science* is not a precisely defined term and scientists themselves differ as to what they emphasize about being scientific. In addressing a newly formed group, the Society for Scientific Exploration, as reported in the *Smithsonian* magazine (Wiley, 1982), Dean Henry Bauer of the Virginia Polytechnic Institute examines these questions of definition and emphasis. Bauer argues that most often science is used rhetorically to signify either power over nature or simple truth. Neither signification is likely to foster attitudes, practices, and ends appropriate to teaching the multitude of subjects for which power over nature is not the aim and in which truth is neither simple nor scientifically verifiable. In the communal judging and testing of the individual's work, Bauer notes, we arrive at "the science that is independent of the individual's style." This independence of an individual's style, its disappearance into something called "science," is at the opposite end from that bringing out not only of the teacher's individual character and style but also of the student's that distinguishes teaching.

Bauer acknowledges, as anyone must, that the "careful, cautious, and repetitious" in science exist side by side with an admiration for the "creative, daring, surprising, and elegant." So, too, in regarding teaching as a science or in emphasizing the scientific study of teaching and learning, one does not rule out the creative and elegant. Still, an emphasis upon methodology, on working toward small but verifiable results, seems to invite the pedestrian, shifts attention away from the vitality and complexity of relationships between human beings. At an extreme is the seductive power of technology and its attachment to science.

Certainly there is a useful technology serving scholarship, and aspects of technology useful to teaching and learning. As I am dismayed about research professors who treat research into teaching and learning disdainfully, so am I toward the automatic disdain that some professors display toward technology. At the same time, I am suspicious of the dreams of technological zealots to turn over learning entirely to technology. My fears are not those of being displaced by the machine but of further displacing from education human beings as more than computerlike functioning parts. The faddishness of the demand for "computer literacy" is created by the attractiveness of the technology in itself and by the promise that something easy will take over the difficult tasks of thought. Some of these thinking tasks can be taken over, are being taken over, but scarcely an instance can be brought forth in which what we may learn by the superior operations of a computer does not feed into complex thought and decision making by inferior human beings. As it is with the linking and decision making that follow from the processing of any mass of data, so it is with the thinking and decision making that follow from the deployment of any educational technology. Insofar as technology is linked to science, perceiving teaching as a science may increase the tendency to see education as primarily aimed at acquiring technological proficiency.

In one respect, at least, I would like to see more teachers display a thorough respect for attitudes associated with science. I have spent much of the last ten years arguing with professors in all disciplines about such matters as grades and motivation, student evaluation and faculty performance, and the relationship between lecturing and learning. In most of this talk I have been on the side of science, the one to argue from what careful investigations have been made rather than from my own experience and bias. I have also argued that college teachers have an obligation to be guided by these more scientific investigations even into "soft" areas of science. Resistance to both arguments has been strenuous and probably as much from professors in the hard sciences as from any others.

Student evaluations afford an example of how even those most sworn to respect scientific evidence disregard such evidence when it does not conform to their prejudices. No corner of the university, including the physical sciences, lacks faculty members who fulminate against student evaluations with little or no examination of the large body of research, chiefly from the behavioral sciences, that underlies the practice. A typical example is a letter from a professor of biological sciences to the *Chronicle of Higher Education* (Jan. 19, 1983, p. 33), denouncing its giving space to an article carefully reviewing recent research into student evaluation. More culpable still was the publication by *Science* (September 29, 1972, p. 1164) of a shoddy piece of research purporting to establish the sweeping claim that "Students rate most highly instructors from whom they learn least."

There is another side to student evaluation in relation to perceiving teaching as a science. An unwise reliance on the quantitative and statistical does a disservice to the complexities of teaching. Such measures may yield useful partial data, as grades give similar limited data about students' learning. But valuing only that which can be quantified in both teaching and learning would keep a teacher from developing any of the larger dimensions of teaching by which a larger learning might come about.

In general, the demand for exactness and certainty associated with the "hard" sciences rests heavily upon the social and behavioral sciences and in turn upon teaching. The so-called soft sciences have modeled much of their inquiries on those of the physical sciences and have been measured by the kind of results expected of the physical sciences. Physical science as a term has too much appropriated the whole of careful, methodical, objective, replicable inquiry, as if before or outside the physical sciences no one framed hypotheses carefully, gathered evidence, compared data, and reached rational conclusions. This kind of inquiry can characterize the soft as well as the hard sciences, the work of poets and politicians as well as physicists. What further needs acknowledgment is that the social and behavioral scientists must proceed on less certainty than physical scientists — as measured by replicable quantitative results — and in greater cognizance of and impact upon the individuals and society under study.

An obvious but vital difference between the behavioral and physical sciences is that the former work with human beings and their immaterial as well as material manifestations whereas the latter confront the nature of matter. However these two may ultimately be one, the way of investigating them differs in crucial ways. We are not at liberty yet to impose the kind of experimental laboratory investigations that are commonplace and indispensable for the physical sciences. Our sense of humanity, let us call it, keeps us from, say, taking babies at birth, setting up a control and experimental group, depriving the one of sensory stimulation through infancy, and then comparing what we have at age three or seven or fifty-five. Clearly, such a procedure, replicated by independent investigators, would yield much knowledge about the relationship between sensory stimulation and mental development. We must, however, make do with such near examples as actuality provides, often forcing the research to make after-the-fact conclusions on less than satisfactorily controlled data.

Much of what can be done within the framework of the physical sciences is inappropriate to the essentially human interactions at the heart of teaching. And too much is left out if one is guided only by what can be quantified and sedulously repeated. Even as teaching may fit among the soft sciences, its firm identification there assigns it to a lesser place in the hierarchy of knowledge. Teaching suffers enough from its lesser status among those preoccupations that seize the attention of university professors; it has little to gain from being regarded as a "lesser" science.

Is Teaching an Art?

Art and craft are closely related terms, craft applying to lesser skills or emphasizing technique, art referring to a higher degree of creativity or creative achievements lying beyond technique. A philosopher colleague of mine (Granrose, 1980, p. 24) has labeled the basic skills of teaching — "choosing, preparing, speaking, listening, responding, testing, grading" — the "lesser mysteries" of teaching. The details that go into developing these skills he calls the details of one's craft. But my friend also refers to the more advanced skills of teaching, which he calls the "greater mysteries." When he discusses this topic, his attention turns toward "developing a certain wholeness of character from which the details of one's teaching will flow. As Nietzsche wrote: 'Giving style to one's character — a great and rare art!'" (p. 29–30).

Whereas I accept dimensions of teaching that go beyond acquiring technical skills, I have some few reservations about dwelling on teaching as an art. I fear that such identification may delude teachers into thinking there is no craft or that paying attention to craft will compromise their aspirations to the heights of art. If all teachers were by nature artists, they would probably recognize the complexities existing between craft and art which are part of an artist's struggles. But art has about it a rarity that may separate being an artist from such a commonplace activity as being a teacher. On the one hand, there is much to be praised about posing the highest kind of ideal for teaching; on the other, there is some loss in entertaining loose conceptions about one's art while craft goes unattended.

Teaching in higher education, as in the public schools, requires great numbers and variety of teachers who must work with other than idealized college students. Thinking of teaching as a highly developed craft may foster more acceptance of using and respecting the materials at hand rather than useless fretting about the materials one would like to have. The gap between one's own highest achievements in a scholarly discipline — one's art, so to speak — and what might best be taught students is very wide. Indeed, as college professors approach the singularity associated with artists, their withdrawal from teaching is an expected outcome. Some eminent scholars are also gifted teachers, but their teaching customarily narrows its range as their scholarly eminence increases.

If we look at the highest reaches of university professing, a related condition appears to compromise the art of teaching. Though there are great teachers in eminent institutions, it is the presence of great scholars that gives universities their eminence. Moreover, great scholars and great artists are seldom found in the same person. Leonardo da

Vinci might come close to being both, but the very diversity of his genius would have made him suspect in many modern university departments considering him for tenure. Practicing artists, now an accepted part of a university's distinction, may also be very good teachers. But like the scholarship that wins eminence, the artists' art is connected with what they do as artists rather than with how they perform as teachers.

So while I would like to see the art in teaching recognized and more teachers who were indeed artists in that art, I fear the confusion of terms. Although the analogies of teacher and artist, teaching and art, fit up to a point, they do not fit exactly. Art finds its way into museums, and we may have enough museumlike teaching without encouraging more. Most artists' pursuits are solitary and lonely, whereas teaching is essentially social and outgoing. And though I have spoken of forming and shaping students as part of a teacher's responsibility, I fear the forming and shaping that might arise from the intense preoccupations of the artist, necessary to fashioning art objects but perhaps unsuited to the broader shaping of human beings.

I do not urge any of these reservations very strenuously. I am attracted to perceiving teaching as an art if only because I find it attractive to be considered an artist (though I am fairly certain I am a teacher). And that may be the point: to recognize teaching for the grand and eclectic thing it is (or can be), and develop it by whatever means we can. For some, it may develop by the application of science, searching and rejecting and verifying, exercising constant curiosity and a tenacity to have curiosity satisfied. For others, it may be by one of the supposed routes of artists, a developed trust in a more intuitive grasp of both a subject matter and student learning. For still others, it may be by accepting the distinction of being an honest craftsman trying to practice an honest craft.

5

Conflicts Between Scholarship and Teaching

Scholarship in many departments of a college or university exists in a somewhat uneasy relationship to teaching. Though ideally the two are harmoniously and necessarily related, in practice they are as wide apart as the phrase "publish or perish" claims them to be. The fit is better for those in the sciences, just as the range of teaching there is narrower. But all professors talk about scholarship quite apart from their teaching and commonly speak of getting rid of students in order to get back to their own work.

Scholarly Productivity

Studies of scholarly productivity, generalized across all fields, reveal clearly identifiable kinds of professors. The majority, fairly early in their careers, fashioned an article or two but have not written a book, have received some kind of grant or another, have received or will receive tenure. Most of these spend most of their working hours teaching, preparing for teaching, or meeting with students and faculty in matters related to teaching. This same majority, early and late in their careers, will both work and play at scholarship. When they fill out those vexing workload forms that some university systems require, they will check off twenty to thirty hours a week spent in research, swelling their working hours to sixty or seventy, impressive evidence of professional commitment. Examining these figures more closely and differentiating between beginning professors and the securely established, one guesses that a good deal of fudging goes on in the numbers submitted. Some part of even honestly recorded hours are more ritualistic than productive: the return to the laboratory at night on a regular basis, for example. Is this escape from domestic tedium or a true absorption in scholarly pursuits? Among humanists, who do not need laboratories, the fashion is to work at home. Certainly in my own department, few offices are ever occupied at night or on weekends; increasingly, many are occupied but little during the working day. Circumstantial evidence indicates that the show of work at home is more for claiming a tax deduction than for producing estimable scholarship. I would go further and say the after-hours work of professors is more likely to be the grading of papers and preparing for classes than the producing of articles. Such honorable if routine work lacks the market value of scholarship; so does the kind of discursive reading or study that cannot be entered in a bibliography.

Scholarly productivity can be fairly perceived as a great pyramid, the work of a very few appearing conspicuously in the upper air, the work of a larger but still small minority apparent in the upper blocks, the work of most down at the base. The king is buried within; few have seen him, most have a superstitious respect that has kept them at it, driving or being driven to do their part. The monument stands, as do the pyramids, as some testament to what human beings can collectively accomplish, some embodiment of the power of worship, social coercion, and economic necessity.

But even this basic building-block analogy is faulty. In theory, much menial work at the base supports crowning achievements at the top. In practice, few great achievements in any discipline are put together quite that way. A more accurate analogy would be a scattering of odd and small-scale assemblages over a great plain, from which now and again some more clever mason will fashion something of beauty or use.

To test this hypothesis just a little, simply pull down from the shelves in any university library the bound copies of theses and dissertations. What a vast piling up for so little use! To pose a more strenuous test, apply to all disciplines the careful study (Cole and Cole, 1972) made of the use of research articles in the field of physics. In actuality, these researchers found that the work used by the producers of outstanding research is itself produced by a small minority of scientists. They estimate that 50 percent of all papers produced are the work of 10 percent of the scientists. As to the work of the other 50 percent, it apparently gets very little notice. "About one-half of all the papers published," Cole and Cole write, "in the more than 2,100 source journals abstracted in the SCI (Science Citation Index) do not receive a single citation during the year after [they are] published" (p. 372). Of the articles appearing in 1963 in the *Physical Review*, the leading journal in physics, about half were cited once or never in the SCI for 1966. This is not to deny that any discoverer stands, as Newton said of himself, on the shoulders of giants. But it is to say that few of the great number of living professors are or will be such giants.

What scholarship is produced in bulk will come from young scholars, not merely because of youthful vigor and quickness of mind, but because of the necessity to publish not only in order to achieve tenure but also to come up to the expectations placed upon them by their profession. At best, most of such work is provincial, the amplification of a dissertation for a highly specialized journal to which conscience may or may not lead contributors to subscribe. Considering the few hundred subscribers for a majority of journals, even conscience of this kind is not very active. Scholarly productivity varies across disciplines as it does from university to university. Nevertheless, one careful study of data (Blackburn, 1982) generalizes that scholarly productivity among a cross section of producing faculty peaks at the assistant professor level, declines during the associate professorship, rises again at the beginning of the full professorship, and declines thereafter. The pattern is not surprising. Sufficient work must be done at the lower level to meet the minimal requirements of scholarly productivity, just as another measure of scholarly work is required to attain a full professorship. For many, I suspect, meeting these minimum requirements is a way of earning the freedom to teach or to use one's mind more engagingly or to pursue more ambitious and far-ranging scholarship, or to expand one's social life. Boredom probably also turns the academic person who has achieved some security away from building-block productivity. Scholarly writing lacks style, individuality, and general interest. Academic scholars who have a facility for publishing master quickly the formula required and, if they persist, doom themselves to an essentially repetitive, hence boring, task of writing and thinking to a pattern and within the secure but often dull bounds of an exhaustively explored area. My picture is distorted; zest and excitement are to be found in scholarship as are utility and, less commonly, beauty. Pearls are found in oysters. But again, I suggest an empirical test for the validity of my basic claim. Read the contents of a handful of specialized journals in any area over a year's time. The enlightenment will be small, the excitement and beauty sparsely distributed, and the wearisomeness marked.

Teaching and Scholarly Productivity

Teaching itself, for all the lamenting about its being valued less than scholarship, exerts a claim upon the majority of professors that helps explain the decline in scholarly productivity that accompanies rising in rank. The necessity of carrying out mandatory scheduled activities, the social aspects of teaching, and the clear superiority one enjoys over students as contrasted with editors of scholarly journals argue for giving teaching the in-fact priority. A day's work done, the strength to turn to the typewriter or return to the laboratory is simply not there for the majority. There is no mystery in this, nor should there be much guilt. Few lawyers function as legal scholars after hours, though they may work long hours wrestling with the difficulties of a case. Doctors, like other professionals, must keep up with advancements in their profession, but they escape to those pursuits they enjoy on days off and during free hours rather than to obligatory research.

As for professors, many are constrained to think they should be producing outside hours, should be engaged in scholarly research, however it may be little related to their teaching or even to keeping broadly abreast of their field. Few can be found who will not speak of work in progress, perpetually and incompletely for most. And few, too, who do not compromise their actual teaching by this burden of being or appearing to be productive. Such compromises include shifting one's teaching hours away from the prime time for doing one's scholarly work (and most likely away from the prime time for students' doing their scholarly best). Or the curriculum can be altered to accommodate a professor's specialized interest, the aims of an established course bent to serve the professor's current research. Scholarship can settle for the easier task of doing a paper for a conference, or wangling an invitation to be a panelist without having to do a paper, or setting up a conference of one's own — all documentable evidence of scholarly productivity that makes legitimate claims on travel funds and bonafide reasons for absence from the classroom. The most baneful result of indulging in such compromises is the self-delusion that one could really be a great scholar if he or she were not burdened with students.

Among a minority — the stars on any faculty — are those who produce much, early and late in their careers. What they produce may include some of those stunning accomplishments of enlightened inquiry; in the main, their productivity will have substance and will justify their position as professors apart from their work as teachers. And yet, many of these are not the movers and shakers within a discipline, and their scholarly work is likely to be as little read now or in the future as the dissertations they sponsor. Teaching remains an important part of their professing, but for professors who achieve the highest degree of success by these measures, teaching loads shrink, students become largely those directed toward replicating their professors' accomplishments, and much of what is taught becomes vocational even though the vocation may bear a professional label. Again, there are exceptions — professors who continue to function in part as charismatic teachers whose teaching aims at some direct contribution to the broad education of large numbers of students, as well as journeyman professors whose teaching is animated by continuing scholarship albeit of a modest kind. Nevertheless, two generalizations hold. The first is that at the upper end of the profession, which embraces those most fruitfully and productively engaged in scholarship, a comparatively small portion of that intelligence and imagination affects the teaching program of a college or university. The second is that though college and university teaching does rest upon continuing scholarship, the kind of scholarship many professors are conditioned to do contributes little to teaching.

At the opposite extreme from the very productive professors, and constituting a much larger group, are those who have never produced much, will not produce much, and thus probably pay the penalties reserved for functioning at a conspicuously low level. One penalty is that they probably have to teach more. If we grant that there may be some connection between scholarship and aptness of mind and fertility of imagination, then we are forced to conclude that, as regards this group, a substantial amount of teaching is being done by faculty of modest or partial competence. If we distrust altogether the connection between productive scholarship and excellent teaching, we are still faced with speculating about the adverse psychological impact upon those who teach a great deal but who have not measured up to one of the central demands placed upon a professor. Given the number and kinds of courses that more successful professors have escaped from teaching, the chances of having too much to do and of a routine but necessary kind are great. Further, such low-level work is not rewarded; promotion is slow and budgets are held down by equating productivity with salaries. Add the absence of opportunities for recognition, change, travel — the small perquisites successful academics enjoy — and you increase the chances of large numbers of chronically overworked and disaffected undergraduate teachers.

The members of this group are easily identified. Many are women; many have come into college teaching from lower schools; many are forced to accept an associate professorship as their highest achieved rank; many have come from undistinguished graduate schools or have undistinguished records in major ones; most have little voice in the shaping of the curriculum or the educational goals or the philosophy of the institution in which they teach, despite the large number of students who are their responsibility. Like those stellar performers from whom they are most distant, individuals in this group may teach well or poorly. But the conditions under which they work, like those different conditions that draw professors at the top away from teaching, are not conspicuously favorable to the overall quality of teaching within a college or university.

Such, in brief, is how I think it actually may be between much of university scholarship and teaching, a description at least as accurate as one that sees no conflicts between the two. Approached from the perspectives of what is necessary to scholarship, academic teaching positions may chiefly provide the freedom and leisure that seem necessary to great achievements of the mind. One of the greatest distinctions of American universities is the number of eminent researchers who have been sheltered there and without being placed under heavy teaching demands.

The "joys of research" are eloquently documented in a book by that title that came out of the Smithsonian's celebration in 1979 of the centennial of Einstein's birth (Shropshire, 1981). These essays, however, all speak to a necessary disconnection between the routine demands of teaching and the highest levels of research. "Science," Einstein wrote, "is a wonderful thing if one does not have to earn one's living at it. . . . Only when we do not have to be accountable to anybody can we find joy in scientific endeavour" (Shropshire, p. 22).

Quality and Quantity in Scholarship

From 1969 to 1971, I directed a project to improve college teaching, which enabled me to visit dozens of campuses and question hundreds of faculty and students. The most consistent response of faculty to the question of how best to improve college teaching was "Improve the reward system." That meant make the system of retention, promotion, and tenure more favorable to teaching, which probably meant — take some of the heat off faculty to be producing, publishing scholars. I have some sympathy with that view, not because I am confident that teaching will be improved thereby, but because of deep suspicions about the quality and uses of academic scholarship. Setting medical research aside, where university-based research may have succeeded most is in developing an increasing capacity for blowing ourselves and our world to smithereens. Even as regards medicine, such an acute observer as Hardison (1981, p. 97) writes: "The history of medicine in the last century is anything but a history of continuous progress. Each major advance has caused problems and crises that have required the abandonment of old values and the creation of new ones; and as medicine has progressed, the process of destruction has begun to outpace the process of creation."

Where academic scholarship has succeeded least — that is, as measured by impact on the larger world — is, say, in the humanities, where the lofty and difficult task of civilizing ourselves has been passed over in favor of glutting libraries with unread works which must be catalogued, kept, and used to feed the workings of an organism chiefly engaged in feeding on its own innards.

If that seems extreme, let me draw some supporting data from my own disciplinary association, the Modern Language Association, and its efforts to keep abreast of the facts of academic publishing. Pell's

(1973, p. 639) summary account of the situation from 1954 to 1973 made this point: "Lavelle's study accurately reflected the situation in 1965. Journals were increasing at a rate soon to be considered alarming; costs were continuing to rise, even more drastically than before; the quantity of material was, in the opinion of some, too great for even the increased number of journals to handle; and, most important, worried grumblings were being heard from many quarters about the quality of or indeed the need for much of the material. The problems Lavelle's article points out are those that the profession faces today, eight years later. They are even more urgent now, and there is no real sense of where solutions lie. The responses of many of the editors to the questionnaire for this survey seem to indicate the profession is facing the problems with much gloom and not a little despair."

Today, ten years after this article, the situation has worsened, though the signs of gloom or despair are chiefly among new Ph.D.s struggling to get something into print that might get them any kind of job. Academics with jobs still feel the larger satisfactions of placing an obscure article in an obscure journal that just happened to come into being in time to provide another step up the promotions ladder. With the depressed market for Ph.D.s and a rising disregard for the humanities, the proliferation of articles and journals may even be viewed by some as a sign of vitality.

In Pell's 1973 survey, the number of journals stood at 216. In 1971, a grand total of 43,932 submissions came in to these journals. About 33,000 of these went to the 127 journals established by 1965; the rest, some 11,000, went to the 89 that had been established within five years. Half of the subscriptions to these journals are library subscriptions, and librarians faced with cuts in budgets and this glut in every discipline are justifiably gloomy. As to quality, one might argue that with a rejection rate of about eight to one, a high degree of quality was being maintained. Having asked editors about quality and having been on the editorial board of a number of journals, I must conclude that much of the material published is marginal, even within the peculiar requirements of a specific journal, and the bulk of what is submitted does not deserve publication anywhere.

Pell's (1973, p. 643) concluding remarks support the argument I have been making here: "Money and subsidies notwithstanding, the editors' and press directors' concerned responses indicate that perhaps the profession should reconsider the publish or perish philosophy. To some, publish and perish are poisoned, wicked words; but, the survey reveals, they are very much a part of academic life in English and foreign-language departments at the present time. In the view of a significant number of editors and press directors, the philosophy is in large measure responsible for the proliferation of second-rate material on topics that interest few."

In surveying the state of scholarly publishing in 1982, Winkler (1982, pp. 21–22) gathered together a good sampling of responsible scholarly opinion. The report of a National Enquiry into Scholarly Communication, sponsored by the American Council of Learned Societies in 1979, had as one of its recommendations that "further net growth in the number of scholarly journals be discouraged" (Winkler, p. 21). Despite such a sensible recommendation and others like it in the last thirty years, *Ulrich's International Periodical Directory* charts a continuing growth from 28,000 titles in 1965, to 57,000 in 1975, to 63,000 in 1981. "There don't seem to be any penalties for publishing a bad journal" (p. 21), wrote Michael West, professor of English at the University of Pittsburgh. The last word on bringing a rule of reason into this aspect of scholarship was probably said by Elliott Berry, a professor of medicine writing about the "journal explosion" in the sciences. The hope of limiting journals, he wrote "will probably turn out like any kind of birth control" (p. 22).

Some additional light on the actual nature of academic publishing comes from the field of psychology. Two psychologists (Ceci and Peters, 1982) conducted a study of peer review of articles submitted to scholarly journals. The method was diabolical but consistent with practices in the behavioral sciences and scrupulously carried out. Thirteen recently published articles that had already appeared in top psychology journals were stripped of their authors' names and university affiliations — all from the most prestigious universities — and resubmitted with changed titles, authors, and university affiliations. All then carried names of unknown authors from low-status institutions. All presumably went through routine editorial reviewing processes. Of the thirteen, only three were detected as being resubmissions. Of the remaining ten, nine were "recommended for rejection resoundingly," and by twenty peer reviewers. The authors' careful conclusions are available to any scholar taking an interest in this aspect of scholarly productivity, though they faced approximately two years of "an intense and negative reaction from many powerful individuals in our profession for having conducted the study."

My point in citing this study here is to emphasize both how touchy professors are about examining the particulars of academic scholarship and how suspect the relationships are between the quantity, quality, and ultimate purpose of much that is published. "Publishing in peer-reviewed journals," these authors wrote (p. 47), "seems to be at the heart of the tenure process, especially for university-level academics in the social and physical sciences, but also in business, humanities, education, and allied fields. Teaching, outside research support (which itself is highly correlated with publications), departmental service, and national professional service (e.g., site visitor, committee membership) are, for the most part, secondary in importance to the impact of one's peer-reviewed publications."

Research and Scholarship

I do not intend to disassociate scholarship from teaching, but rather to ask that academicians ponder the nature of both and to question many of the assumptions about both that underlie academic values and practices. I accept scholarship as a necessary part of teaching but plead for *scholarship* broadly interpreted to be maintained as the word rather than *research*. Research is surely a subcategory of the many ways a human mind seeks understanding of the world it occupies. Because of the practical success of science, however, research long ago fastened itself upon the university as that which every faculty members should — must — do. It is both an inappropriate term and, often, a lower-order mental activity. Let me illustrate again from my own field, English. Research is inappropriate to most of what we do, though the discipline is as occupied with it as if it were a laboratory science. Inappropriate, in the first place, because few institutions in this country have the resources for significant primary research into fresh and important literary documents. Second, major philological investigations, which were the beginnings of research in language and literature, have been done, and they cannot be done again in that same sense of original research. Third, few first-rate literary minds give first priority to literary research, though a good novelist may have to find out about many things, and some very good research scholars are also writers of distinction. English, one might say, is a peculiar example: clearly, its highest values are attached to writers and their creative works—Shakespeare, Chaucer, Homer, Aeschylus; its next highest values are probably toward critics, though a Dryden is not a Shakespeare nor is a Henry James, critic, a Henry James, novelist; somewhere below that are the philologists and bibliographers and linguists and of late semioticians and structuralists. Fourth, despite, in major research universities, universal pressure to publish, the great majority of published work comes out of a minority of scholars. Moreover, in one responsible survey, though faculty members in English said their major satisfaction came out of teaching, they also said their major professional responsibility was research. Finally, within dwindling graduate programs, institutions like my own have maintained their health because of the large numbers of graduate students opting for a Ph.D. in one form or another of creative writing. If that is not enough evidence for the unreal place research occupies in the real world of teaching English, or even professing it, consider that English is once again in the public eye, as it has been in the past, not because of some one or another stunning research accomplishment but because the public is concerned with its—and the university's—inability to teach students to write.

This last observation brings out the narrowness with which research is defined in English as in other disciplines. Following a Germanic, scientific model, American universities have always had a fondness for theoretical research, "pure" as against "applied." Research into how human beings learn to write and the application of such findings to teaching is still a marginally respectable activity for graduate work in English departments. Similarly, the teaching of writing is a responsibility thrown upon graduate assistants and lower-rank faculty. Graduate assistants who might be usefully assisting graduate professors in their research, if that research included how students learn to write, are instead employed as laborers whose daily work is far removed from the kind of research either they or their professors are doing. Somewhat similarly, the writing of poems and stories and plays was until recently rigorously excluded from graduate work in English largely because of the emphasis on research. Only shrinking enrollments in conventional Ph.D. programs, a large number of undergraduate students turned on to creative writing, and an increasing demand for teachers of such courses have forced creative writing to become a legitimate pursuit in a significant number of graduate schools. Academic departments cling tenaciously to narrowly conceived models of what should distinguish graduate study. Even within the so-called hard sciences, the narrowness is somewhat suspect, and where there are practical ends—bioengineering or computer applications—the marketplace breaks down academic conservatism.

If the term *research* is inappropriate for much of what English professors do, it is even more inappropriate for other human activities brought within the university system. The university, as a major patron of the arts, has had to modify its reward system with phrases like "research and creative activities" or "in lieu of publication, artistic works may. . ." Even performances have been made acceptable. A music department that has secured the services of, say, Yehudi Menuhin, tolerates his concertizing, does not tick off the articles he has placed in the American String Research Association Journal nor count the grants he has obtained to investigate the comparative vibratory properties of stub-tailed or long-tailed cats' guts.

If a distinction could be made even between research and scholarship, and if expectations placed upon faculty members could be defined both more generously and precisely, large numbers of professors might have a better fit between what they profess to do and the work they actually perform. I am not opposed to scholarship, only to the narrow definitions placed upon it. A teacher should know or be able to do something very well in order to assume the role of professor. Let us loosely call this "knowing" and "doing" scholarship and speculate about what might be sought after if scholarship is to be linked more tightly with teaching.

Linking Scholarship and Teaching

Appropriateness, which I have discussed with respect to English, is a vital consideration in all the disciplines. While it is vital for some—not all—physicists, chemists, and engineers to have laboratories, equipment, and perhaps teams of workers, it does not follow that clinics, laboratories, or even equipment are appropriate for education or history or philosophy departments. We must establish within the university, among our colleagues, a recognition of the various scholarly activities in which our many and varied departments engage and respect for the particular services they perform. A first order of business, then, is to widen the ordinary opportunities for faculty to become acquainted with the variety within their university. Interdisciplinary teaching and learning is no less a necessity for faculty than it is for students. Moreover, interdisciplinary scholarship— not formal research—is a similar necessity. Yet, the impediments to both are large. I have heard few strenuous arguments against interdisciplinary work and many affirmations of its desirability and attractiveness, but interdisciplinary work has had hard going from the time that the various disciplinary associations were formed. Similarly, I have never heard any arguments against the usefulness of professors in one field getting together with professors in another. Yet, the separateness in which professors live their lives, closeted within departments and even within subspecialties of departments, in small colleges as well as large universities, is one of the most disturbing aspects of places that call themselves either colleges or universities. Until faculty are willing to find out about what goes on elsewhere in the university, to educate themselves in this way, many will continue to suffer under a reward system that imposes upon them narrow views about both scholarship and teaching.

Not only must the faculty become acquainted with the diversity that characterizes a modern university but they must also shift their values to be consistent with this wider perspective. The closest example that comes to mind is the importance attached to writing and mathematics skills. In the abstract, such skills are highly valued by an entire university faculty. Graduate professors are as quick to lament the deteriorating ability of students to write as are beginning instructors who must actually deal with such supposed deterioration. Faced with such evidence as falling Scholastic Aptitude Test scores, even the faculty in the sciences come forward to lament the decline in literacy. In the current wave of anguish (only the most recent of periodic spasms), some headway is being made to make writing a university-wide responsibility. Still, even where this movement has had some success, the majority of professors take no active part in it. A more conventional and comfortable response to deficiencies in writing skills has been to blame the secondary schools. It follows that raising college entrance requirements is the way of "getting *them* to do their jobs." Such reflex gestures give cursory attention to the complexity of causes and largely ignore what is known about the acquiring of writing skills. Disclaiming any personal responsibility, the professors turn back to their own protected domains. In the avowedly scientific disciplines, writing in any demanding sense is neither practiced by the professors themselves nor exemplified in the journals in which they publish, nor fostered in their classrooms.

Of the many causes for students who cannot write as well as professors think they should, surely two are that the professors themselves practice poorly what they preach and that they play only a small part in the actual instruction of writing. It is a university faculty, supposedly acting with collective wisdom and knowledge, that assigns writing to a limited number of entry-level courses within a single department and then condones that department's relegating of instruction to teaching assistants and low-level faculty. It is a university faculty that looks with suspicion on any faculty member who by choice or assignment has made the teaching of writing a central professional concern. It is a university faculty, acting through its graduate research preoccupations, that casts doubt upon the value of practical research in the learning or teaching of writing. It is the separate departments and colleges of a university faculty that will not surrender hours in their vital subject matters to increase composition requirements and that do not value writing enough to teach it as a part of any department's major responsibilities. And it is the university faculty members who countenance writing within their disciplines that is bad by any standard of literacy that has existed in the long history of English prose as public discourse.

Necessary changes being made, much of what has been said about writing could be said about mathematical literacy. Clearly, teaching basic mathematics earns as little reward and recognition as the teaching of composition. Clearly, there is very little in-fact reinforcement of the need for mathematical literacy across the university. Clearly, the teaching and learning of mathematics is no respectable interest for mathematics professors wanting advancement and recognition. If there is any major difference, it is probably the general ruthlessness with which mathematics departments flunk out large numbers of students and then lament, along with their colleagues in the sciences, student aversion to science and the general low level of scientific literacy. The curious myopia reveals itself in a discussion of "the decline in mathematics skills" at the 1982 meeting of the American Association for the Advancement of Science, as reported in the *Chronicle of Higher Education* (Trotter, 1982). The university professors cited identified the problem with teachers, students, and attitudes in the public schools. No attention was given to the teaching of mathematics in the university or to the development of public school mathematics teachers, despite statistics that 22 percent of high school teaching posts in mathematics in 1981 were vacant and 26 percent filled by teachers who were uncertified or only temporarily certified in mathematics. Until faculty members are willing to modify the singular value attached to their most pretentious and hypocritical claim — that they are all and, of a right, should be working at the frontiers of knowledge — and acknowledge the value of much other university work, the universities will continue to turn out great numbers of technically trained graduates basically illiterate in one or more fundamental ways.

Though I will not charge mathematics or science with responsibility for the preoccupation with quantitative measures that exists in the university, I will argue that scholarship must, to some degree, be broken away from the mere doing of, piling up of, research. As regards the teaching faculty, the mere counting of articles and citations deserves the hostility it has aroused. What I would ask for is more vigorous and specific examining of the intellectual activities of a faculty member as they have outcomes in teaching. *Breadth* would surely be a measure here, as against the besetting narrowness that describes most of our scholarship. *Connectedness* would surely be important, particularly at that point where scholarship must connect with the students, as contrasted with the usual measure of connection with colleagues. *Valuing* is a third necessary criterion. That is, scholarship must ask value questions, including "How much is what I am doing worth doing?" Promotions committees have not begun to establish criteria of this kind, nor to seek ways of examining them. Failing to examine scholarship in these, rather than the received ways, faculty will continue the present uneasy and unsatisfactory relationship between scholarship and teaching.

Finally, *cooperation* need gain a larger place, as against the present competitive, free enterprise model. Departments must function as part of the common enterprise of educating students who are human beings before and after they are engineers, English majors, or physicists. And faculty members within departments must be engaged in this common enterprise rather than being purely the twelfth-century English history specialist or the turtle zoologist or the social stratification expert. There are strong social attractions in the linking of scholarship and pedagogy that might help offset the fact that much scholarship is a solitary activity. And there is also scholarship in pedagogy itself, the curious and probing mind finding out more about teaching and learning just as it investigates a subject matter, but with this difference: such scholarship would necessarily involve the cooperation of the human beings it seeks to understand as well as affect.

Changing Perspectives Toward Teaching and Scholarship

Despite the strong liberal arts collegiate tradition, present-day colleges and universities are so influenced by the size and prominence of research universities that little can be expected in arriving at a better balance between teaching and scholarship. Nor is a faculty, pressed as it has seldom been before by an unfavorable academic market, capable of doing much to reverse the tendency of that very market to increase the necessity to publish. If we but had administrators who were informed by other than parochial views and who were willing to exercise the powers they have and the leadership they might exercise. If we but had institutions that represented more than the diffuse self-interests of the faculty and expedient responses to immediate public pressures. If we but had a culture less susceptible to values based on higher and larger. If we but had students more resistant to a faculty's tendency to replicate themselves and to carry out an institution's pressure for productivity. Even then, we would still not be free of the scholar-teacher's individual and collective self-interest.

For there is a great personal attraction to heaping up and getting higher, quite apart from any specific pursuit and as applicable to scholarship as to making money. Knowing more is easier when followed along a congenial line and within manageable dimensions. Specialization not only pays off — virtually all professional athletes are specialists, not only in one sport but within that sport — it can be gained early and leave time for other pursuits later. Working with the mind has a higher social value among the totality of jobs, probably a higher monetary value, than working with things or people. As the future according to Andy Warhol would give everyone an instant of fame, so it promises everyone professional status of a sort. All this goes against being just a teacher and particularly being a teacher possessed of both a broad learning and a broad competence in affecting students. The individual's urge to be a professional, which implies being a specialist — physicist, historian, cosmetologist — is overpoweringly strong.

At a practical level, the forces against teaching's being informed by a wider view of scholarship and practiced within a milieu awarding full value for teaching in itself are just as great. Hawkins (1979, p. 285) has well described the earlier struggle of research to win a place beside teaching in "the new and newly shaped institutions that revolutionized American higher education in the last third of the nineteenth century." The scholarly disciplinary associations founded during this period rest on traditions going back to the classical past. Present American collegiate institutions reflect a century of expanding and building upon a European model that has achieved tremendous success of a kind. Within these structures, a bureaucracy is in place that operates on machine-tooled replaceable parts distributed across the nation. No vice-president or dean is likely to be put in place who does not look remarkably like his predecessor. Chairpersons and division heads reflect the faculties from which they come. Presidents, whose selections are not as tightly controlled by the inner bureaucracy or faculty, still must fit the pattern of trustees overwhelmingly accepting of the university as it is rather than as it might be. Looking ahead toward the end of the century, demographic patterns promise no vast increase in student population that might affect some change in perspectives toward teaching and learning.

The issues behind the functioning of scholarship and teaching are larger than their manifestations in academic attitudes and practices. The furthest reach of these implications is survival itself, that to be addressed in the next chapter.

6

Questioning the Value of Knowledge

*T*he relationship between scholarship and teaching has more serious implications, though harder to come to grips with, than those discussed in the previous chapter. Chiefly, these have to do with the religious respect that a knowledge society, as ours is sometimes called, has toward knowledge. Within the institutions devoted to knowledge, its pursuit is the one unquestioned value. The graduate schools are its ecclesiastical centers and graduate professors its priests. Its theology is as dogmatic as that of medieval scholasticism and probably less torn by disputations over subtle points.

Were we sure that we had arrived at the final view of truth, we might be as secure as scholastic theologians were in their view of truth and the way of going about pursuing it. But the events of this century must create doubt about the absolute value—much more, the survival value— of that truth. In the first place, there is the inescapable fact that we have a command of energy that can destroy earth's civilization, if not the physical earth itself. We also have faced, since World War II, growing evidence that crucial natural resources will be depleted and possibly within the lifetimes of many of us. Related to both is the paradox that war will become ever more destructive and ultimately unmanageable despite the spread of reason and the expansion of knowledge.

The response of intelligent and knowledgeable human beings is split. One group argues that knowledge advancing further will find new resources, will make the leap from this planet to another, either to enhance life on earth or to extend human life elsewhere. Another group, equally serious, argues for the necessity of acknowledging our limitations, adapting ourselves to conditions that all our reasoned intelligence cannot change. The scientist René Dubos (1981, p. 244) concludes: "Science and technology provide us with the *means* to create almost anything we want, but the development of means without worthwhile *goals* generates at best a dreary life and may, at worst, lead to tragedy." My purpose here is to charge the university's scholar-teachers with the necessity of raising fundamental questions about knowledge itself.

Tenets of the Faith

If, as I claim, modern society views knowledge with religious awe, accepts a theology of knowledge, what are the tenets of this faith? Fundamental is the idea of the advancement of knowledge as the one supreme, self-justifying activity for mankind. That idea has had a long run, at least since the time Francis Bacon opposed scholasticism, and has had tremendous success in the accomplishments arising from systematic and unfettered inquiry. Bacon shared with other humanists of the Renaissance the belief that advancing knowledge would not only bear fruit but would also be a means of breaking away from idol worship, religious tyranny, and despotic government. The freedom of the human mind is a grand concept set ringingly forth in Jefferson's "eternal hostility to any tyranny over the mind of man."

Compelling as these ideas are, we still must question the basic premise that the pursuit of knowledge is of such unqualified value as to preclude continuing and searching scrutiny. Though there has been continual criticism of the nature of schooling in this country, there has rarely been any fundamental questioning of the idea of schooling or of the extension of schooling. In the fifties, there were vigorous debates over the question of who should go to college and on the advisability of extending the community college system. The issues were never really settled; rather, social forces in the sixties brought into being both an extension of public schooling into the first two years of college and a great growth and strengthening of graduate education. Both competed successfully for public and private financing because, in part, both were supported by a secularized religious faith in knowledge.

Though anti-intellectualism has frequently manifested itself in American education (Hofstadter, 1963), it has never checked the steady growth of formal education nor the expansion of products of the intellect into American life. Paradoxically, species of anti-intellectualism live by the very intellectualism they preach against: the trained intellect is very good at serving anti-intellectual desires. What else does one make of the rock group Pink Floyd belting out "We don't need no education" through tens of thousands of dollars of sophisticated amplifying equipment to be heard through hundreds of millions of dollars of receiving equipment? Human beings go on inventing automobiles, light bulbs, television sets, and computers, all of which serve as much to extend our physical and sensory pleasures as to expand our minds. The counterculture of the sixties, rendered quaint in a scant dozen years, seemed for a time to coalesce various anticognitive, antischooling, antiscience and technology gestures into shaping a new attitude toward knowledge. Still, little transformation of basic perceptions toward knowledge has taken place. Within the university, the retreat back into the received modes of pursuing knowledge is marked.

The assertiveness of the right to follow knowledge wherever it leads, to support in the realm of thought the same free marketplace that one associates with political democracies, is a strong characteristic of university scholarship. Teachers stoutly defend similar freedoms in the classroom. Nevertheless, both may have to bend to limitations upon personal freedom in the pursuit of knowledge, somewhat as the society of this planet has been forced to recognize the planet's physical limitations. The contrast between the physical expansiveness of the world in Bacon's time and the closing of frontiers in our own plays a part in questioning such a compelling idea as freedom of inquiry. Faced with the questions of survival, the supposedly unfettered pursuit of knowledge might give way to one less governed by individual choice but also promising to bring to bear more of a society's intellectual and imaginative energies on matters of first importance. At the least, scholars and teachers might more clearly acknowledge that their work, even now, is governed by a great many forces other than the restless curiosity of free men.

The examination I am proposing is no easy one to make. Throughout history, questioning the value of knowledge and imposing limits on freedom of inquiry have been associated with behavior of which know-nothingism is one of the least objectionable manifestations. But the history of the twentieth century is full of atrocities committed in the full light of enlightened inquiry and expanded knowledge. I wish not to be misinterpreted here. Examining the values we hold, even the value of knowledge, admits of every degree of probing. We may need to pay more attention to those — albeit their numbers historically embrace some strange and wonderful types — who have opposed an almost exclusive devotion to systematic rationality and the knowledge that arises from that devotion.

Questioning Other Articles of Faith

There are other articles of faith, basic assumptions many professors make about knowledge and the ways it should be pursued, that also need scrutiny. Four of them are: (1) that knowledge is quantitative and structural; we contribute to it as well as discover it, and we build upon previous knowledge; (2) that knowledge yields only to highly specialized pursuit; in itself it is value free, its worth assessable only by specialized pursuers; (3) that knowledge primarily, if not exclusively, submits to and is advanced by objectively demonstrable acts of cognition, systematic rationality conjoined with empirical verification; and (4) that knowledge is superior to knowing, that one can deal meaningfully with knowledge without consideration of knowing as a process in which the subject's knowing is important as well as the object known. Without pushing the religious metaphor further, let us consider these tenets and speculate about their effects upon scholarship and teaching.

First, what of regarding knowledge as a "stuff," packageable, quantifiable, structural, and the like? A host of evils arise from this hard-to-escape premise. As organisms we move from less knowledge to more. As hard as it is to deal with knowledge as a concept, it is easier to deal with amounts than kinds. The effects within formal education are obvious. The grade and credit system is a quantitative system. The awarding of degrees, tied as it is to courses completed, knowledge supposedly accumulated, is also quantitative. Wherever one turns, knowledge is wedded to education as being kind of a vast currency, not altogether different from the treasury of the medieval church, from which one gets credits and vouchers, which purchase social grace, physical well-being, and clean work. All of these are hard to avoid. Try, if you will, to conceive of other than a quantitative knowledge. We have, of course, made distinctions in kinds of knowledge: sacred and profane, the black arts and fine arts and applied arts, the hard as against the soft sciences, and humane learning as contrasted with technical know-how. Yet in practice, all of these get quantified.

I am not proposing to lay bare the falsity of our regard for knowledge as a commodity and to propose the right way of looking at it. But at least we need to question the common assumptions about knowledge that figure prominently in the transactions of formal education — for example, that all knowledge is sequential, additive. That assumption is strong even in humanistic studies, which, until recently, were conducted almost exclusively along chronological lines. Scientific studies, which tend to slight history, still firmly embrace a sequence of necessary progression in almost all disciplines. Educational practices from lower to higher are locked into sequential patterns: having acquired this knowledge, students can go on to other knowledge, or not having this knowledge, they cannot go on. Education primarily takes place in the amassing of disparate pieces of information over a period of time within formal structures which both define knowledge and the proper ways of pursuing it. The value we attach to producing and heaping up knowledge as a commodity support an educational system that is rigidly hierarchal. Professors are above schoolteachers; producing knowledge is superior to disseminating it or applying it. All of these value assumptions would be challenged by the college or university professor whose teaching was not compromised by the received truths of modern scholasticism.

Our educational efforts are affected in numerous ways by the individual and institutional acceptance of these and related values. We are, for example, caught up in a knowledge explosion, a further extension of the quantitative metaphor. It is a curious metaphor, for though it seems to acknowledge a danger — explosions blow people and things to bits — it actually poses more discomfort than threat. To those engaged in the production of knowledge, the explosion metaphor adds some excitement to quiet pursuits, but knowledge remains a basically benign substance, capable of being controlled, deployed, and piled up to the betterment of everyone.

Knowledge as a stuff supports a second article of faith to be questioned: that the production of knowledge yields most to highly specialized pursuits, and that the quality of production can only be judged by the specialized knowers. University faculty members do spend some of their time debating what, for students, is most worth knowing, though such debates are as much characterized by departments and individuals arguing to get a piece of the pie or protecting maximum hours in the major as by educational principle. At the graduate level, these questions are seldom asked. Of the individual professor, the questions are more about producing within an accepted field of specialization than about the value of such productivity within the larger worlds of either scholarship or teaching. As the graduate school catalogues put it, the scholar's highest aim is "to make a genuine contribution to knowledge," to put something into the treasury. The professor's duty, sacred duty if you will, is to embrace, add to, some bin of knowledge, a particular bin because knowledge is so vast and disparate a stuff.

Moreover, in all the appointing and evaluating the university does, the framework of specialized knowledge that creates departments and colleges and disciplines resists all attempts at valuation of what is going on except by those who accept the values of specialized knowledge. In many universities, judgment of a faculty member's worth is heavily weighted by turning over assessment of productivity to the outside specialist. Why should not such judgment favor work of a colleague wise enough to choose that specialty and prudent enough not to invade another's territory or question his work? The qualities of teacher, which cannot depend upon the momentary attention of one specialist to another specialist's scholarship, must struggle to be recognized and valued.

The deferring of judgment to the specialist's opinion strengthens the tendency, already strong, to regard knowledge, particularly in the form of fact and number, as value free. Reducing the scope of one's inquiries may indeed lead to a kind of certainty and purity that rises above uncertain and impure human values. Out of an intensity of vision, a fixedness of purpose, comes much of value in what we teach and learn. And yet, by the same route one arrives at a trivialization of scholarship, a constricted teaching, which are indeed value free because so little of value can be attached to them.

A third article of faith is that knowledge primarily, if not exclusively, is advanced by objectively demonstrable acts of cognition, conscious acts of perception and mind aimed at facts, theories, concepts, and other manifestations of systematic rationality. No one could examine the youth scene or the university catalogue today and claim that noncognitive approaches to knowledge are not present. But the recognition of more than one mode of knowing, one kind of knowledge within the formal educational program, is little more than a gesture to capitalize upon the popularity of the supernatural or irrational among students. Cognitive knowledge is still dominant, despite widespread frustration with that dominant mode's ability to provide answers or to provide some measure of content despite a lack of answers.

The mating of systematic rationality with empiricism has been undeniably fruitful for the sciences. Perhaps its success alone explains why, within the university, the methods of science and its heavy emphasis upon cognitive knowledge have dominated all areas but without the same appearance of unqualified success. By now an unimpassioned analytic study of literature has done more harm to poetry, defined in its broadest sense, than a vaporous appreciation may have done in the past. I see no great superiority in the assertion "I like what I know" over "I know what I like."

There are those who will argue that cognitive knowledge is the university's peculiar and prime concern; therefore, as it strays away from that preoccupation, it betrays its purpose. The growth and the nature of growth of undergraduate and graduate education in this country make that a hard position to defend. As institutions now directly affecting the lives of a majority of the population, the colleges and universities have clearly accepted wide responsibility for fostering all manner of sciences, arts, professions, and even crafts. Despite the continuing presence of conservatories, business colleges, and trade institutes, there has been no resisting the attracting power of the university. The multiversity, like it or not, is the central institution of American higher education. These institutions, despite their encompassing nature, still act as centers of a universal faith, still support a single creed tied to the superiority of cognitive knowledge, and still exercise constraints over those who fail to adhere to the creed. If that were not so, surely graduate schools would have developed or maintained various certifications to distinguish the many pursuits of mind and heart and hand that are worthy of advanced study. But the interest has been in upholding the faith, preserving the purity of the Ph.D. degree, rather than in risking the rise of other gods, other creeds. The gravest consequences are that the graduate school, in its specific preoccupation with one mode of knowing, turns out great numbers of uneducated men (and a few women) who become the supposed educators of an increasing number of the general populace.

The final article of faith to be questioned is the denial of knowing as a process in which the subject's knowing is as important as the object known. In sober fact, we may only *know* something through the skin and, even then, only know it fleetingly while the pain is intense, only have any real grasp of it through a Kafka-like penal machine embedding the message in needles on naked flesh. Within the framework of reconsidering scientific knowledge, Polanyi (1958) has tried to establish an alternative idea of knowledge, what he calls "personal knowledge." "I have shown," he writes, "that into every act of knowing there enters a passionate contribution of the person knowing what is being known, and that this coefficient is no mere imperfection but a vital component of his knowledge" (p. viii).

Granting the importance of cognitive knowing, I still feel uneasy over the slighting of other ways by which we move to knowing in a profound sense — where the word *knowledge* is no longer adequate, where something like understanding, growing in wisdom, becomes more precise. My point, trimmed of all qualification, is that knowing is but a means to an end or ends, and cognitive knowing only one means. If that were clearly recognized within the practical world of education, learning would be a more various, less pride-enslaved, less channeled and confined, and maybe, even, a more joyous activity. Most important of all, students would not end up with the shallow instrumentalism which defines their acquiring of supposed requisite knowledge and skills to embark on careers. They would gain some awareness through the awareness of enlightened teachers that there is more to a satisfactory life and to a society that functions well than knowing things as the university has defined knowledge.

What is most troubling about an excessive valuation placed upon cognition is that it makes its own practices less accessible to examination and correction and that it limits the exploration of other ways in which we might become knowing. Oakeshott (1962, pp. 197–198) writes:

> The view dies hard that Babel was the occasion of a curse being laid upon mankind from which it is the business of the philosophers to deliver us, and a disposition remains to impose a single character upon significant human speech. We are urged, for example, to regard all utterances as contributions (of different but comparable merit) to an inquiry, or a debate among inquirers, about ourselves and the world we inhabit. But this understanding of human activity and intercourse as an inquiry, while appearing to accommodate a variety of voices, in fact recognizes only one, namely, the voice of argumentative discourse, the voice of "science," and all others are acknowledged merely in respect of their aptitude to imitate this voice. Yet, it may be supposed that the diverse idioms of utterance which make up current human intercourse have some meeting-place and compose a manifold of some sort. And, as I understand it, the image of this meeting-place is not an inquiry or an argument, but a conversation.

Conversation — surely there is a metaphor which, if really pursued within the formal structures of education, even within the social sciences and humanities, would produce different students, different attitudes toward vital public questions, than the kinds that prevail now. Nor am I talking about "conversation" in some genteel, donnish way. I am talking about it as encompassing the toughest kind of talk for facing the ugliest of our situations. And I am talking about it as different from knowledge stored up in, to be learned from, the ordered systems of written symbols upon which our present knowledge and education depend. We must heed the warning in Lèvi-Strauss's statement (in Charbonnier, 1969, p. 30) that "writing, in the first instance, seemed to be associated in any permanent way only with societies which were based on the exploitation of man by man."

Mistaking the Furthest End of Knowledge

There is much that is faddish about the rejection of technology, of the values of the university, of systematic rationality. Similarly, doomsaying has become something of a vogue. But it is too easy, too comfortable, with most university professors pretty much captives of the rational mode into which they were educated, to see any strange phenomenon as only momentary. There still may be some possibility that events, if not conscious choice, will bring about powerful changes in our basic perceptions of man's purpose on earth and his way of following out those perceptions. A physicist from India discussed with me the honor accorded to "wisdom" in his part of the world; still, as a physicist, he said, he embraced my Western world's belief that the highest aim of man was "the intellectual comprehension of the world." It strikes me that this goal established itself in Western civilization as a replacement for the "intellectual comprehension of God." As the earlier aim aroused an excess of spiritual pride, so our latter-day one arouses an excess of material pride. Neither one nor the other is free from the delusions, idols, and vanities of learning.

"I have been touched," Francis Bacon wrote to James I at the beginning of *The Advancement of Learning*, "yea and possessed with an extreme wonder at those your virtues and faculties which the philosophers call intellectual; the largeness of your capacity, the faithfulness of your memory, the swiftness of your apprehension, the penetration of your judgment." Thus, that indispensable aspect of modern science, grantsmanship, began. Bacon's *The Advancement of Learning* (1968) was more than a proposal; much of the first part was an assurance to the king (whose sapience, as Bacon described it, should have needed no assurance) that divinity had placed no real curbs on man's advancing of learning, that learning threatened neither God nor man, and that true learning has often been disfigured by the faults of men.

Bacon concluded his critique of false learning in this way:

> Like as many substances in nature which are solid do putrefy and corrupt into worms, so it is the property of good and sound knowledge to putrefy and dissolve into a number of subtile, idle, unwholesome, and (as I may term them) vermiculate questions, which have indeed a kind of quickness and life of spirit, but no soundness of matter or goodness of quality. This kind of degenerate learning did chiefly reign amongst the schoolmen; who having sharp and strong wits, and an abundance of leisure, and small variety of reading; but their wits being shut up in the cells of a few authors (chiefly Aristotle their dictator) as their persons were shut up in the cells of monasteries and colleges; and knowing little history, either of nature or time; did out of no great

quantity of matter, and infinite agitation of wit, spin out unto us those laborious webs of learning which are extant in their books. For the wit and mind of man, if it work upon matter, which is the contemplation of the creatures of god, worketh according to the stuff, and is limited thereby; but if it work upon itself, as the spider worketh his web, then it is endless, and brings forth indeed cobwebs of learning, admirable for the fineness of thread and work, but of no substance or profit [pp. 285–286].

The end of Bacon's proposal for advancing learning was to arrive at a new philosophy, for "the greatest error of all the rest is the mistaking or misplacing of the last or furthest end of knowledge" (p. 294).

It is precisely this attention to "mistaking or misplacing of the last or furthest end of knowledge" that should be the scholar-teacher's foremost concern. If we are to move to a new philosophy, we must set out to discover a world we can live in and focus our energies on defining and respecting, and we must use knowledge to shape a world to fit the image of our best selves. The overriding issue is survival, not only in terms of controlling the forces that can destroy or deplete civilization but also of resisting the slower destruction of human communities that enhance living. The fundamental recognition of the coming age may be that we must work within limits that still include a global community. Attractive as the whole range of expansive metaphors has been to Western society (the geographic expansion almost exactly paralleling the advancement of learning), these metaphors may be part of the malady of our times. And as humanists helped chart a course in the direction of these discoveries with the metaphors of voyaging, exploring and expanding, subduing, conquering, and rendering to human use, so humanists now may have to provide new and satisfying metaphors for a harder course. That course may lead away from the essentially lonely, ego-ridden, divided, aggressive, competitive world that lay at the end of Bacon's *Advancement*. A different outlook would so dominate society that new institutions would arise, old institutions change to embrace "community" as a first principle rather than as a secondary principle out of a remembered past. The building of a community rather than the building of knowledge would become a first level of action, just as would making our living space livable rather than finding new places to live. From such an apparent lowering of the value of knowledge would follow changes that heightened almost everything that goes on in the name of teaching and learning.

Teaching for Survival

To bring all this down to the level of teaching and learning, teaching for survival might be described in this way. Structurally, teaching and learning would move much of what is taught out of small packages of unrelated knowledge to a clustering of knowing and conjecturing and relating among professors and students. An easy, if imperfect analogy in automobile manufacture, for example, is the movement from the linear assembly line to the clustering of operations involving larger parts. The aim, quite apart from transmitting information or assembling autos, is to give both workers and students a sense of larger purpose. If one argues that it is dangerous to pose an industrial metaphor for such infinitely complex business as fashioning an educated person, I will only reply that that is the model we now follow and in antiquated forms at that. The access to information afforded by technology has a chance to flourish in such a transformed structure as I describe. For much relatively simple learning, being engaged in gathering information and in acquiring skills to put it to use would be integral to this kind of study. That is, the increased socialization that takes place in the assembling of students and teachers around problems, ideas, quantities of relatable information, would increase the receptivity to self-learning, without which technology is powerless. It would also break through the dominant competitive model to a cooperative model and from a separate learning as an end in itself to the insistent questions of what knowing and doing are for.

The usefulness of multidisciplinary work is recognized among scientists themselves. Wolfle's book for the Carnegie Commission on Higher Education, *The Home of Science: The Role of the University* (1972), quotes Weinberg (1971, p. 314), "The universities fall short because they are fragmented and disciplinary," and Long (1971, p. 961), to make the general point being made here: "But the most important reason why the universities must become involved in interdisciplinary research — and the central reason why society must *insist* on their participation — is their obligation to youth. Coming generations must be taught about society's problems and about the best ways to solve them. College students must learn a genuinely interdisciplinary approach; this can only happen when their professors have personal knowledge of and commitment to interdisciplinary research and when there are programs wherein students can learn by doing—in short, when an interdisciplinary approach permeates the university."

There are great changes in attitudes toward teaching and learning entailed here. The greatest is that of suspending the notion that knowing in itself has any worth and replacing it with a notion that knowing is always in a context that both affects and must be affected to declare its worth. This may seem to dislodge that cherished ideal of knowing for its own sake—as a loosely held notion, much in need of dislodging—but closely examined, it does no such thing. Rather, it places knowing for its own sake in a saner perspective. That is, described in terms of professor to student, it does not say there are things you must know because our wisdom or experience or expertise declares it so, nor does it say you must learn to set aside your own sense of what you need to know in favor of knowing for its own sake. Rather, it says, we live our lives within some crucial and common frameworks—earning a living, establishing a community, maintaining our health, preserving our lives, arriving at a satisfying self-identity; all of what we know or wish to know relates crucially to these. Education is to be perceived in large part as a gathering of people—let us call them teachers and students—to become both more informed about and more capable of dealing with these basic realities as they show forth in a myriad of ways.

To make my point clear, let me juxtapose some present-day ordinary practices as they might appear under a new structure. There would surely be no Introduction to Sociology or similar courses as lecture classes to great numbers of students for defining and conceptualizing the obvious. What there would be are settings which in themselves illustrate social processes and which bring to bear such learning as an economist and social scientist and educator and biologist might marshall if confronted with students for whom some aspect of arriving at a satisfying community was the focus. There would be no flocking to computer departments under the awful threats about what happens to computer illiterates. Instead, the computer would appear as it has appeared in our larger society, to perform a large variety of useful jobs. Computers might become a good deal more common to a student's education than they are now, not because of required courses in a basic skill but through their use wherever certain kinds of information serve the needs of human beings engaged in important human inquiries. What is said here of computers might well be said of other basic skills courses. Physics and chemistry, let us say, might well go on two legs but they would conspire to walk and run rather than to hop as too often they do now. By that I mean, except as we would train physicists and chemists, there is little excuse for the sealing off of a somewhat sophisticated knowledge of the physical world from a majority of college students. In its present practical form, what is at issue is science for nonmajors, one of those academic problems that never get solved, probably because those in the sciences do not really want to move toward very obvious solutions. Here, the present structure having been broken down everywhere, respectable and attractive alternatives to being practicing physicists and chemists open up for the teachers of physics and chemistry.

There is an irony about the shortage of public school teachers in the sciences at the same time that the prestige of sciences in university departments is high and the number of job-seeking students with B.S. and B.A. degrees is large. The conventional reasons are the low salaries and disadvantageous working conditions attached to public school teaching, but other reasons must be brought forward as well. One is that, in the general decline of bright students from Education, students in the sciences are least likely to opt for teacher preparation programs. Another is that within the university, mathematics departments maintain high failure and attrition rates in their beginning courses. Further, it is in the sciences that the attitudes toward knowledge being criticized here most prevail.

While scientists bewail what is to happen to science if science teaching in the public schools is so deficient, faculty members in university departments pay little heed to the complex of forces creating the problem. Students cannot be forced into teaching careers; the separation of science subject matter departments from colleges of education is a long-existing and deplorable fact. Without some prestigious science educators operating as peer models within a department faculty, students are not likely to opt for teaching as a career. The difficulty of beginning math courses is another reality, widely advertised among students. So, in the large universities, is the presence of large numbers of apprentice science teachers, many, in recent years, nonnative speakers of English whose idiom is an additional barrier students must overcome. So are attitudes that neither give teaching high priority within the faculty nor envision teaching excellence as that which might attract students and help achieve low drop-out and flunk-out rates.

The current plight of public school teaching and learning in the sciences is but one of the serious practical effects of a distorted valuing of knowledge. The corrective in this instance has been to provide more fellowships to attract more students to graduate study in the sciences with the hope that some will embrace public school teaching careers. We might as well attract sharks to a bathing beach with the hope that some will turn out to be lifeguards. What is most appalling about forcing great numbers into advanced study is that so much of it sucks up human intelligence and imagination into a supposed advancing of knowledge while the spread of essential knowledge—upon which advancing knowledge ultimately depends—remains a marginal activity. Put more bluntly, one first-rate public school teacher doing nothing more than turning on hundreds of students to science and mathematics is worth several dozen average Ph.D.s turning out articles for specialized journals.

As structures would alter to provide contexts for learning related to larger ends, so teachers' perspectives would alter to see students in these contexts rather than in the context of their own specialized ends. Most of what I might say here is already established in the emphasis placed upon style and character in the beginning chapters of this book. For the society that glimmers out there, the one an abundance created by technology can provide, depends fully as much on the creation of a population willing to have such a society. I will set aside my own skepticism about Utopias and argue from an optimistic futurist's most expansive dreams. The mere acquisition of technical skills does not, I think, fit that dreamer's ideals. So long as we retain an essentially human society, the development of those characteristics that work against man's destructive propensities is fundamental. The teachers with a respect for survival must interest themselves in the development of the student, contribute as they might both to making "becoming an adult a reasonable option," in Csikszentmihalyi's words, and to shaping that adult toward civilization beyond mere survival. Knowing and more than knowing, on the part of the teacher, is involved here. The minimum knowing is that which illuminates how human beings develop and that which postulates how they should develop. Beyond that is a teacher's willingness to make the effort, take the risk, enlarge one's capacities that either verifies knowing or nullifies it.

Finally—not because I have completed a design but only because I have hoped to establish that there can be connections between theory and practice — teachers are going to have to become more selective about their knowing. No paradox is intended here, following as this does an implied expansion of a teacher's competences. Rather, the price of expansiveness may be a greater selectivity within that widened expanse.

I would argue for greater selectivity even were I to see no change within the present attitudes toward knowledge. Implicit in my asking for more willingness to value knowledge is the simple statement that some things are more worth knowing than others. In theory and in practice, one could argue, the universities are now and have ever been engaged in selectivity about knowledge. What else is there in the debates about core curricula and programs for majors and high school solids and computer literacy? But one could as easily argue that the present curriculum, whether that of a single department or of a university, discloses rough selectivity as best. And even in those times when the "best ever thought and expressed" was a more operative principle than it is now, that selectivity was both narrow and wide — as narrow as the bias for Western culture, as wide as whatever in Western culture attracted a human being's interest sufficiently to turn it into an academic subject. "If the world does not always make sense," Frederick Rudolph has written, "why should the curriculum?" (1977, p. 2). My interest is not to pursue this debate, only to establish that the selectivity about knowledge apparent in universities does not embrace my precise intent.

What I am saying has a much more disagreeable tone, for it asks the scholar-teachers to wrest the selection of what they give their minds and hearts to out of the packages of knowledge found in their disciplines, out of the paths of self-interest (even survival of a kind) that choose computer technology over eighteenth-century poetry because of its job potential, and even out of the contexts that the advancement of knowledge has provided. In this self-examination, there would be an acceptance of the difference between what we may like and what we value, what we would have and what society might need. And to make the charge even more disagreeable, the individual selection would make itself felt in institutional ways. Fields of study might well disappear, not by supposedly "natural" attrition but by conscious choice as they are measured against the larger need — the survival of civilization.

Perhaps none of this is called for; we will survive or perish unmindful of what we know or do not know or how we go about knowing.

The intensity with which I argue, and without any great certainty of pointing the right way, grows out of a belief that survival is at stake. I have heard few assertions as chilling as that of the sociologist John Seeley (1969, p. 71): "Western civilization lies all but dead under its own learned knife."

It is to be acknowledged that the sixties brought forth, in Europe and here and among intellectuals around the world, much questioning of systematic rationality. But there is little coherence in that questioning and it probably aroused more resistance among the faculties of academic institutions than acceptance. Michel Foucault's views arise from these questioning impulses of the sixties. It is not surprising that his individual studies of how organized systems of knowledge exert power should lead to his efforts "to expose and specify the issue at stake in this opposition, this struggle, this insurrection of knowledges against the institutions and against effects of the knowledge and power that invests scientific discourse" (1980, p. 87). Serious philosophical and political intents underlie Foucalt's work, though as it is embraced within academia it has the familiarity of heretical doctrine springing up within any theology and which keeps doctrinal disputes and those who live by their presence energetically engaged.

These and other heretical ideas make their impact, but within the accepted lines of academic inquiry, recognition, dissemination, and power. As large minded as they appear to be, in practice they tend to become the property of specialists within recognized academic disciplines. I see little hope that they will bring any large numbers of academics to ponder such a meditative question as Lindbergh's (in Dubos, 1981, p. 244): "Does civilication eventually become such an overspecialized development of the intellect, so organized and artificial, so separated from the senses that it will be incapable of continuing functioning?" There is some hope that teachers in their living contact with skeptical students genuinely anxious about survival may perceive such questioning as central to the conduct of their education and lives.

7

Seven Deadly Sins
of Teaching

The corruption of institutions is not surprising to anyone with a knowledge of history. Nor is the corruption of individuals much more than an admission of human imperfection. Though modern intellectualism has questioned the very idea of sin as a useful concept, the presence of sin, whatever it may be called and however it may be regarded, is as obvious in our time as in any past era. Academic novelists are fond of portraying venal professors, just as analysts of faculty politics remark about the viciousness of the conflict considering the smallness of the stakes. But teaching, as I have been arguing, plays for very large stakes, and the theological bent of the last chapter has turned my mind to considering sins we teachers commit, sins as deadly to students' chances of learning as the traditional deadly sins were to chances of salvation.

As I see them, the seven deadly sins of teaching are Arrogance, Dullness, Rigidity, Insensitivity, Vanity, Self-Indulgence, and Hypocrisy. Pride is clearly operative in most of these; Sloth should probably be included, though, like Lust and Anger, I will leave it as more appropriately among humankind's general sins. I am not arguing for professorial exclusiveness here; sin is such that, however we classify it, there is plenty to go around.

Arrogance

Arrogance is a very common sin of young professors, particularly those who come from famous places and arrive at humble colleges. Like any prolonged incarceration, the experience of graduate study may not so much humble its survivors as leave some bent in the direction of humiliating others. Quite apart from the tendency of a once-subjugated class to seek revenge, knowing something someone else does not know is an invitation to arrogance, manifested in playground taunts as well as in questions on Ph.D. orals.

There are three common kinds of academic arrogance. The first arises from the nature of specialized study that places very large amounts of information in people of very limited experience. For many beginning professors, schooling has been their chief involvement, affording too few first-hand experiences with all kinds of excellence that might put specialized academic expertise in some perspective. Having missed the experiences of rubbing against more of the raw stuff of life, a person inclined to excessive pride may magnify the worth of certified professional status.

The result may be a teaching stance that has a kind of chic appeal: the newest professor with the "smarts," as the lingo goes. Colleges and university departments tend to capitalize on the prestige new faculty members bring with them from their more famous graduate schools. If, as often happens, dazzling intelligence is accompanied by a boorishness of manner or studied seediness of dress, the impact is just that much enhanced. Given the nature of graduate schools, a new professor may already have picked up mannerisms that range from a faint distaste for what one is doing but doing it nobly to conspicuous bullying that calls upon a variety of histrionic powers. Even in the face of resentment from large numbers of undergraduates who, like other human beings, are put off by arrogance, an arrogant manner sufficiently well displayed may win a coterie of admirers.

But classroom arrogance can arise from another source, insecurity, for which it is the commonest of defense mechanisms. The arrogant manner shuts off embarrassing questions, protects the young teacher's shaky skills, and limits close contact with students not much younger and maybe brighter than their teacher. Its manifestations are the tightly controlled classroom with the nonstop lecturer at its center, the put-downs when questions do arise, the arbitrary exams, the savage and sarcastic comments on papers, the assigning of too many tests and too much work, and an exaltation of subject and discipline that squeezes out any consideration of other learning, other aspirations, other smarts than the professor's own.

For all that American higher education has close relationships with democracy, its scholarly character is borrowed from aristocratic traditions. Its beginnings in this country were clearly associated with educating a small portion of the populace. Admissions standards still mark this elitist character, made even more marked by the high tuitions that go with high prestige. Where one has gone to school carries a stronger sense of social position in America than any other single sign. All of these cultural forces operate on college professors coming out of graduate schools where academic hubris is most pronounced. Having the wherewithal to attend, the intelligence to meet its demands, and the social position a prestigious graduate school confers—how can one not be arrogant, and of a right?

Still, professors who remain arrogant are wicked teachers and probably wicked human beings. Learning is not a servile activity; that is why all repressive political regimes have suppressed learning ruthlessly or narrowed it into learning to obey. It is possible to beat and shame and terrify whole populations, as well as individual students, into knowing only what they should know. But as for the ordinary effects of arrogance in the classroom, it succeeds, if at all, in a negative way. Smarting from a teacher's arrogance, some pupils extend themselves to prove teachers wrong or show them up. Such passions can last very long times and animate very high achievements. But anger and hatred are, in general, wasteful emotions, for learning as for the attaining of other human satisfactions. Most students facing arrogant professors are not likely to be fired for long even by those passions. Instead, they wait such professors out, drop their classes, bad-mouth them to friends, and most insulting of all, forget who they were or what they taught.

A second kind of arrogance, known more to a professor's colleagues than to students, is an arrogance about one's subject matter. As a humanist, I think scientists are particularly prone to this sin, as they may think that of me and my kind. We are all susceptible to it. Disregard for the public schools, for example, is spread through all the disciplines, and though arrogance about our disciplines is not the sole cause, yet something very much like it must reside in the distance we maintain from those other teachers whose work so closely parallels ours. Within colleges and universities, arrogance of this kind underlies the pecking order among academic departments. The inferior departments in a university are as clearly identified by some members of superior departments as if they were set down by a Universal Academy or a Supreme Foundation. Such arrogance is particularly devastating to teaching, for colleges of education have been clearly assigned to an irremediable inferiority. The ultimate arrogance in this respect, even when it is not belligerently held, is that no one really knows anything much about teaching and certainly knows nothing that runs contrary to one's own limited experiences.

The third circle of arrogant sinners is occupied by the professionally arrogant, scholars driven by their own esteem past mere vanity to a fixed belief not only in their rightness but also in their essential inestimable worth. As a student's rage against insult may drive him to high achievement, so an arrogant professor's passion to prove all others wrong may record some remarkable achievements along the way. Or it may merely result in the tiresome professor whose daily lectures are built around quarrels with scholars whose names mean little to students and whose right-or-wrong theories mean little as well. No true scholar can escape echoing Newton's eloquent pronouncement that he stood on the shoulders of giants, though all may long for the achievement — if not the arrogance — in Pope's dictum: "God said let Newton be and all was light." History affords many examples of arrogant scholars, though their work, when examined in light of even greater scholarly achievements, seldom justifies that arrogance. Many of the greatest of scholars were genuinely humbled by the immensity of what was still to be known, even as they were forced to place themselves respectfully among their betters who had preceded them and who would come after.

The arrogance of the specialized scholar is one explanation for the lack of fit between scholarship and teaching discussed in Chapter Five. I do not mean the display of vanity, which is another kind of sin. Arrogance comes forth in the tenacity with which the highly successful scholar refuses to acknowledge the full worth of a vast, unsorted, unspecialized, unacademic learning that distinguishes human intelligence and imagination. Carrying such banners as "excellence" and "mind" and "rigor" and "discipline" and "standards," archangels of arrogance occupy high positions in the highest of universities and fasten their limited design on all lower education.

The complexity of learning invites arrogance in the system builders who initially believe they can reduce complexity to order and terminally believe that they have done it. However modestly urged, a system that purports to explain all learning behavior, whether embodied in a development theory or in a teaching methodology, courts arrogance. As such systems — and Marxism and Freudianism can serve as other illustrations — go beyond the originators, they have an often fatal attraction for the insecure, who need such frameworks, and for the ambitious, who can use them to build their own careers. The single-minded, often passionate, acceptance of such limited conceptualizations of truth does lead to the arrogance of any believer in dogma. Possessing the truth, even if its central tenets embrace humility and brotherhood, believers set themselves above the nonbeliever. Their solicitude for others is that of any missionary: to effect another's salvation, an act of great if disguised arrogance, it seems to me.

It is possible, even necessary, I acknowledge, for some scholars to develop valuable systems, and for others to use such frameworks, embracing them arrogantly. The various embraced and discarded systems that most affect pedagogy — Lancastrian learning, behavioral objectives, operant conditioning — make their point and yield to the multiplicity and complexity of teachers and learners and learning. Teachers cannot avoid being caught between an acceptance of the multiplicity of things and an urge to see them in some order. All I am citing here is a commonplace of sin: its outward attractiveness and its promise of inner satisfactions. That the arrogant cannot perceive the mix of truth and falsity that resides in the systems they proselytize is testimony to the powers of the Old Deceiver.

Dullness

Dullness is a seemingly benign sin, yet it competes with Arrogance for the highest (or lowest) place. Like other mortal sins, deceit over what it is allows it to prosper among the virtuous. Many professors argue its partial virtues: much learning is by nature dull, or all learning cannot always be fun, or what is dull for the student may be startlingly interesting to the rest of humankind. Moreover, dullness breaks no bones, works no violent crimes like murder or assault. And yet it does break spirits, does turn spirited youth into plodding hacks, and does turn many promising others away from academic pursuits. However seemingly gentle its ministrations, there is violence in its coercive powers, forcing human beings to submit to regulated boredom by the constraints of curriculum, grades, degrees, and careers.

Unlike the arrogant, the dull often maintain their positions because of the defenses put up by their colleagues; they, themselves, are often too dull to notice their dullness. The defenders, who may not be dull teachers themselves, are nevertheless conditioned to a certain level of dullness, and bring forward such compensating virtues as an immense command of fact or capacity for work or absence of positive harm worked on students. The humaneness that flows through these defenses belongs among humankind's highest social virtues, somewhat as attacks on dullness tend to be regarded as uncivil, even "waspish." But dullness in teaching should be looked at for what it is and for its effects before it is defended. There is something awful, sinful in the extreme, in inflicting one's dull self upon another for an extended period of time from which the other has little chance of escape. Thus perceived, it is not so different from physical assaults punishable by law. No ordinary citizen is permitted to hold another in bondage for even fifty minutes a day, subjecting such person to physical assault and extracting a fee for the privilege. True, the cover of "consenting adults" excuses a wide range of barbarous behavior, though in the ordinary college, many of the victims of dull professors are not yet adults and many more cannot be called "consenting."

Only the fact that it leaves behind no physical marks, no welts and bruises and lacerations, has kept enforced dullness from being included among capital crimes. I reason, even now, from memories of sitting through the wearying dullness of numerous classes and the even duller reading of papers at professional meetings. What great abuse dullness heaps upon students daily and under coercion not only to survive but to derive some benefit from it!

It is necessary to make this point strongly, else the lesson as regards teaching and learning will be lost. For attention and interest are not just important to learning, they are near everything. Dullness not only disregards the need for attention and devalues interest but also excuses inattention and destroys interest. Over the years, it has forced upon one of the most inspiriting of activities — learning — an association with that most dispiriting of human conditions — being bored. With institutional support and faculty acquiescence, dullness has often been equated with profundity; dull professors have been accorded a depth and solidity that makes them safer bets for promotion and tenure than their more interesting counterparts. Finally, it has added greatly to the confusion about what students can and can't, will or won't, might and don't, learn. Faculty chronically confuse a dullard's specific lack of professional competence — an inability to motivate learning, to raise and sustain interest — with students' lack of background, appreciation, or intelligence. There are, to be sure, dull students. There are dull subjects. There are dull institutions, and dull stretches of the day and season. But a teacher is or should be professionally skilled in combatting all those dullnesses that stand in the way of active learning.

Nor are shortcomings in this respect to be excused because higher pursuits should not be sullied by the kind of hawking in the marketplace that constantly tries to claim our attention. To reject all the ways by which one gains and holds attention because they have been put to use for meretricious ends is to reject everything that might mark the beginning of learning. And yet, some such rejection probably helps explain the graying out of academic work as contrasted with the more exciting life promised (if not found) on the American college campus.

The nature of academic dullness, the techniques even by which it is achieved, deserve more attention than they are given. Even writers, often the victims of dull schoolmasters, do not convey the most stultifying aspects of dullness. It is difficult to be dull in short space, and a pedant's precise dullness would have to be precipitated out of other offensive but provocative behaviors. A teacher's dullness needs conveying not only by words on a page but also by the experiencing of mutter and stumble, drone and clichés, bearing and posture. Dickens's *Hard Times* does about as well as any book to catch varieties of pedantry and boorishness in Mr. Gradgrind, Mr. McChoakumchild and Mr. Bounderby. Pope's *Dunciad* created a Queen of Dullness and her company but nevertheless ended up as a dull poem for most readers. A section of Book IV suggests a kind of academic dullness that still abides:

Plac'd at the door of Learning, youth to guide,
We never suffer it to stand too wide.
To ask, to guess, to know, as they commence,
As Fancy opens the quick springs of Sense,
We ply the memory, we load the brain,
Blind rebel Wit, and double chain on chain,
Confine the thought, to exercise the breath;
And keep them in the pale of Words till death
(IV, 11.154–160).

Rigidity

Rigidity and dullness often occupy the same academic body. Rigidity may be the lesser sin, if only because it offers some resistance for a student to push against. Dullness seldom asserts, almost always acquiesces. But although rigidity may get the student exercised, it seldom grants satisfaction. Faced with a rigid teacher, the student has little choice but to opt out, do it the teacher's way, or pay the teacher's price.

As a sin, rigidity is rooted in the denial of freedom to others, the fatal corruption that goes with power. Rigid teachers use the same rationalizations as do tyrants everywhere: they know what is best for those over whom they have power. Sometimes professorial rigidity does serve the student's real interest, just as arbitrary rules often save someone time and trouble. But for learning which moves in many and mysterious ways, rigidity serves little purpose. Embraced by a teacher, it stands in the way of responding to the variety of students, the complexity of subject matter, and the spontaneity good teaching demands. Even if it were morally defensible, it still would not be pedagogically wise if the teacher's aim is to encourage learning among a large number of students.

At best, rigidity may simplify a student's choices, including those specific choices about how he or she might best go about learning. Even here, the higher pedagogic skill brings the student to simpler and better ways, not because the teacher has imposed them but because he has inspired the student to search them out. No teacher can escape the necessity of providing discipline, and few are patient with students learning by trial and error. What is missing in the rigid teacher are the pedagogical skills that can discipline without discouraging, indicate ways without prescribing paths, and pose ends and means to ends without keeping students from thinking out ends and means themselves. Human beings develop along common lines but in different ways. Effective teaching and learning are grounded in awareness of that development and diversity. Order and sameness are but ways of rendering multiplicity and difference, for the moment, manageable. The teacher can assist the student to face the swarm and flux and to divine something of its nature and purposes. No one can and should do that entirely and coercively for another.

Institutions do much to force rigidity upon faculty or to provide rationalizations for an individual's inflexibility. Fixed class hours and credits, standardized grading and testing, degree and certification requirements are conspicuous examples of basic patterns to which teachers must conform. Even teachers resistant to regulation may find that conforming simplifies bureaucratic life and often lightens their teaching load. Still, it seems almost an article of faith that a good teacher should not hide behind rules he or she cannot respect. If faculty were more questioning of the multitude of institutional regulations that fall more heavily upon students than faculty, they might create institutions more responsive to individual needs and without diminishing their economy of function.

Insensitivity

Insensitivity is both a sin of omission and commission. As dullness goes undetected by the dull, so insensitivity escapes the insensitive. Judging these sinners by their intentions would leave many blameless. But judged by their effects, insensitive teachers are guilty of causing confusion, misunderstanding, discouragement, pain, anger, and worse. Some teachers may cultivate insensitivity. They may claim to have begun their careers overflowing with sympathy and to have found it necessary to become thickskinned to survive. Or, discovering early that being insensitive shuts out the distractions standing in the way of single-minded success, they may have adopted and cultivated it as a way of rising to, say, an administrative position.

Within a college, faculty in the various disciplines could easily be lined up along a sensitivity scale. Over with the cuddlies are professors of health and recreation, oddly closeted with physical education instructors who have a very peculiar macho sensitivity at best. Engineering hard hats represent more than just protection of heads. As a group, engineering and science faculties have less access to the popular currents of sensitivity than faculty of business schools, schooled by management and marketing to the economic advantages of controlled sensitivity. Male-dominated faculties continue to be a fact in these disciplines and confirm the stereotype that places greatest sensitivity with women and artists.

Prizing cognitive knowledge and the superiority of mind over all else, higher education has traditionally set little store by sensitivity. The senses were the enemy from which a cloistered kind of learning helped the pupil escape. As science became dominant, the senses were replaced by more accurate tools of measurement, the objectivity of the machine becoming the model rather than the subjectivity of the sensing self. Only in the last two decades, and prompted by the messy passions of youth, has sensitivity, awareness, imagination, creativity, expanded consciousness, to use a cluster of terms, gained some attention. The "affective" domain is now recognized as having some importance and place in both lower and higher schooling. Popular psychology, as if in rejection of the mechanical coldness of its behaviorists, washes its readers in wave upon warm wave of sensitivity. College teachers coming into the profession of the seventies can hardly have escaped some contact with the warm feelies, though their younger colleagues and still younger students may have missed the most fervent advocacy of living life at the nerve ends.

As much as the recent passion for sensitivity may be culturally induced, so one form of insensitivity arises out of a preoccupation with self. High achievers may have to sacrifice sensitivity to others in order to fulfill the driving claims of ambition. *One has no time to contend with student problems; my job is to teach my subject matter to the top of my ability and the student's job is to get it. Besides, any proper college or university has a counseling center or department advisers who are good at that sort of thing.* Such bluster does not disguise the fact that the sensitivity outstanding teachers show to students and their learning simply does not matter that much to the ambitious academic driven foremost by personal professional goals. Behind the dutiful carrying out of teaching responsibilities is a valuing of self over others, a lack of equal respect for what the professor does as scholar and what the student may achieve as learner. How the student may develop as person is even more remote from the insensitive teacher's main concerns.

But there is another kind of insensitivity, the bumbling kind that is often seen as excusable, even endearing: the teacher so wrapped up in his subject (as distinct from self) that he is prone to walk into trees. No

more insult is intended to students existing at the margins of consciousness than to the trees. Brought to awareness, such a professor may
express and genuinely feel such sensitivity as can come from those whose
ponderings have cut them off from the sensible world.

Like most sins, insensitivity has its shadings from light to dark.
Sensitivity, in teachers as in human beings, can itself become morbid.
And yet, as I perceive professors and, as well, the administrators many
become, I see insensitivity as not only a sin but also a mark of professional incompetence. For what learning requires in any situation where
interaction between persons is central is responsiveness. The student
achievement that goes unrecognized, the grievance unaddressed, the
questions unanswered, the anxiety unacknowledged, the student left to
brood on the shame of his ignorance — these are venial if not mortal sins.
At its mortal worst is the kind of insensitivity that perceives sensitivity as
an intellectual weakness, a teacher's caring as idle appreciating and emo-
tionalizing, and a student's sensitive life as set apart from the doing of
academic tasks at hand and on time.

Vanity, Self-Indulgence, and Hypocrisy

Vanity, Self-Indulgence, and Hypocrisy are a closely related trio
of sins so much a part of human makeup as to give little hope of correction. Vanity is but the lesser form of Pride, that deadliest of sins because
we would not be human without it and yet, having it, we open the door
to all other sins. I will single out but one manifestation of vanity, that
which underlies the "flight from teaching," as the Hazen Foundation
characterized the behavior of professors more than a decade ago.

Simply put, teaching does not sufficiently feed the vanity of many
professors. The gratitude of students is not enough nor of the right kind.
Were they not ignorant they would not be grateful, and praise from the
ignorant is faint praise indeed. What the vain professor requires is the
praise of colleagues, the recognition of disciplinary peers. In the drive to
produce, vanity is a far more potent force than economic gain. The
printed word spread throughout the academic world satisfies professorial
vanity in ways that teaching cannot.

Vanity, like most Christian-based sins, places the demands of self
above the demands of others. Teaching, however, by its very nature, is
always asserting the demands of others. What the student requires is

often in conflict with what the teacher would rather have. One common professorial response is to inflate a limited and highly specialized subject matter into a course required of some or all students. Vanity may attach such importance to the teacher's current research that students become the captive audience for daily reports read from the printed text so as not to miss a word. Examinations conducted by vain professors are often, for the student, exercises in psyching the professor out. From the student's point of view, vain professors are manipulatable but touchy, even role models of sorts, a means of measuring one's own need for flattery and sensitivity to reproach. On balance, the conspicuously vain professors are not easy for students to come to terms with and are the cause for chronic complaints about favoritism and other kinds of imbalance and unfairness and trivializing.

Thirty years of living among academic men and women have convinced me that we are a self-indulgent group, albeit we purport to be in service to others and accept an income that does not permit us to be as conspicuously self-indulgent as some other professions. We insist on being our own bosses, yet we treasure the security of salaried positions. We insist on shaping our teaching to fit our convenience and resist its being shaped to anyone else's. We condone a kind of sloth that often masquerades as great busy-ness. We publicly lament our modest incomes but privately use them to justify our absences and lapses and attention directed elsewhere. Given modest support for the scholarship that underlies teaching, we often squander what we have and lament not having pushed for more. We do not, as a profession, push ourselves very hard; collectively, we fight against pressures to produce but we do not produce as much as summers freed from teaching might lead one to expect.

I will not claim to be describing the profession as it exists for every professor and at all times. Self-indulgence may seem to be a callous term to apply today to a young Ph.D. competing with a half-dozen other young Ph.D.s for a tenured slot in a major university. And yet, whether that young professor secures the spot there or finds another permanent position down the scale, the career at either offers temptations to self-indulgence. As one succeeds at the high end, so do the perquisites increase that go with academic success, chiefly the granting of financial support and released time to pursue those activities that the self finds most gratifying. Most often, the amount of teaching of large numbers at lower levels shrinks, the amount of teaching of students and classes closest to one's heart's desires expands. Once tenure is achieved, no one is going to be pushed very hard for either a steady flow of articles or teaching that is both difficult and outstanding.

What I am citing as temptations to self-indulgence are attractive aspects of professing, incentives for bringing men and women into the profession who might have opted for more aggressive and lucrative careers. Many may still perceive academic life as a genteel profession, best pursued by those with a modest outside competence that allows them to indulge in more refined kinds of self-indulgence than a professor's ordinary salary can provide. Some make up for outside income by having an employable spouse, others by doing a variety of high-paying writing and consulting and contracting open to academics. In the past twenty years, collective bargaining has encroached upon the private nature of a professor's work, bringing into play other forces that place conditions upon the professor's work. By annual negotiations and contractual agreement, collective bargaining moves toward regulating what self-indulgent professors claim as their right: to set their own conditions of employment, to carry them out with a minimum of interference, and to pursue their scholarly bent wherever it might lead and however it might relate to teaching.

At the extreme of self-indulgence is the sin of academic sloth, plain laziness for some, for others a lack of zeal toward the faith that theologians call *acedia*. Slothful habits easily develop in professors who have met the basic demands of minimal teaching and scholarship and who retain no great ardor for either. In any university, the running of the institution, uneasily shared by faculty and administrators, leaves much room for those faculty members who want to be lazy. Teaching cannot be totally avoided, though it can be fit into convenient hours and trimmed to its least exacting proportions without arousing adverse attention. The show of scholarship is easy to maintain. Even easier to shirk is the committee work, the participation in academic governance and planning that is inequitably distributed in most universities. Some of the seemingly slothful are engaged in scholarship of a high order, some are teachers of great excellence whose work escapes attention. Too many, I fear, are captives of their own private indulgences, early off campus to whatever diversions their own sense of talent and worth entitles them to. Even then, the self-indulgent can believe that an instrument of cerebration cannot be answerable to clock or whip; seemingly at rest, it is fully functioning all the waking hours.

The collective self-indulgence of faculty as teachers is responsible for much of the quantifying and packaging and accounting for and certifying that besets teaching and learning. Reform in any of these respects is thwarted by the simple fact that any better arrangements will cost a faculty more than they currently pay. No one has been able to resist continuing proliferation and fragmentation of courses, not just because knowledge is expanding, but because faculty members shape courses and expand the curricula to fit their own interests. Grades will stay despite their inadequacy as feedback and motivation because they are simple devices for the faculty to use. Final examinations, more ritualistic than educational, will loom large because they provide an additional period of time for the faculty to do what they wish. How exams are read, when they are read, or even if they are read, are strictly within the faculty's control. In any obvious sense, students pay little for these sins of their professors, nor do they perceive them as sins. Learning, they have already been told, need not be integral, needs no more than grades and tests to make it go, need not cause anyone any great inconvenience. The faculty has set up things to serve their convenience; the higher ordering of the world has seen to it that it fits the students' convenience as well. Even the self-indulgent practice of turning classes over to a graduate assistant or dismissing them altogether while the professor is responding to some higher call off campus is for the students more a source of relief than complaint.

The best of students, by these measures, will become professors, and many of those will be following a common kind of self-indulgence that keeps one on a path that, however long and arduous, is well worn and defined. Even in these bad times for Ph.D. candidates in many disciplines, their ranks are made up of some with firm and driving ambitions, idealistic at one end and self-assertive at the other, but the larger numbers of those who keep on an academic track do so because of their own temperament and the lack of satisfactory alternatives. Few graduate students would think of themselves as self-indulgent, and, if they are, the wages for such sin are small indeed. And yet, such a faculty as I see coming out of these conditions may turn to self-indulgence as a kind of revenge against the poor prospects that open up to them when they find any academic positions at all. Being forced to take positions at lesser institutions than their advanced work seemed to promise, a current generation of professors may feel justified in taking advantage of that one privilege that still is open to them: a high tolerance for doing as they please.

Hypocrisy, not identified as one of the traditional Seven Deadly Sins but conspicuous in the behavior of Deadly Sinners, exists even in the most moral of collegiate institutions, if only in the rhetoric one finds in college catalogues. The idealistic foundations of most colleges and the materialistic realities they face make some hypocrisy inescapable. College presidents recognize benign dissembling as a prime qualification. A president, for example, must say both that the real strength of the institution is in the faculty and that this faculty in all qualities that count is second to none. In most places, he must convince the faculty that their salaries and benefits are better than those of faculty at comparable institutions but, at the same time, hammer the point home to trustees and legislatures that his institution's salaries are or will be falling seriously behind.

Any president who has managed to live with his institution's big-time athletic program is a master of hypocrisies of many kinds. The faculty is party to the largest hypocrisy: that college athletics are academically respectable and under faculty control. By no measure of honest reasoning can big-time athletics be found compatible with even minimal standards of honest academic work. Nor can, in any honest sense, the army of coaches be regarded as "faculty." The most stalwart of presidents and the least tokenish of faculty members on athletic boards cannot honestly claim to be in control of an enterprise so driven by uncontrollable cultural forces. By no stretch of standards can many of those on athletic scholarships — for example, that portion who do not complete degrees — be regarded as students, nor can the recruiting of athletes be defended as ethical or academic activity, nor the National Collegiate Athletic Association as an academic body. At my own university, one with a reasonably corrupt athletic program, the various basketball classics begin just after Thanksgiving and run through the New Year holidays. During final examination week, members of the basketball team are up to their ears and off campus preparing for and participating in the holiday shootouts. There is neither time then nor opportunity later to do academic work, and the fiction that faculty maintain that somehow intercollegiate athletics has been brought into harmony with academic programs is the most stunning hypocrisy of all.

The most honest words spoken about college athletics probably in decades are those of U.S. District Judge Miles W. Lord (Wehrwein, 1982, p. 5) in a decision ordering the University of Minnesota to admit a basketball player to a degree program.

> We must view with some skepticism the defendant University's claim, regarding academic integrity. This Court is not saying that athletes are incapable of scholarship; however they are given little incentive to be scholars and few persons care how the student athlete performs academically, including many of the athletes themselves. The exceptionally talented student athlete is led to perceive the basketball, football, and other athletic programs as farm teams and proving grounds for professional sports leagues. It may well be true that a good academic program for the athlete is made virtually impossible by the demands of their sport at the college level. If this situation causes harm to the University, it is because they have fostered it and the institution rather than the individual should suffer the consequence.
>
> . . . The public interest is difficult to assess. It depends on whether the public prefers highly tuned athletes who devote most of their waking hours to honing their athletic skills or whether it wants an individual with the plaintiff's athletic abilities to be required to make substantial scholastic achievement. There is no doubt that the public does have an interest but until the universities themselves clarify their position on the matter, the Court must assume that the public interest is equally ambivalent.

If my tone grows harsh in addressing this final sin, it is because the offense is great and long continuing. The corruption of athletics is at the very center of what education tries to do — not to subjugate the flesh to spirit, not to provide nourishment for the mind while all else starves, but to bring some harmony between flesh and spirit. The playing of games in which heart and mind and body are fully engaged is immensely attractive. Team sports, consuming for young participants, are as compelling for spectators of all ages. Why such activities within American colleges are so riddled by deceit and dishonesty testifies to the power of pride and ambition, the continuing war between materialism and idealism, the concrete and abstract, life as it seemingly must be lived and as it might be lived. Beyond the specific abuses is a more frightening prospect, a world still incapable of tempering the effects of force, body, brute strength with reason and compassion.

Dante was wise in having each of the sections of the *Divine Comedy*, even the *Inferno*, end with a view of the stars. In my most mordant fancies, I see one circle of Hell composed of an immense football stadium in which endless contests are being played to empty stands and the most successful of coaches are listening eternally to the most boring of professors and the most hypocritical of presidents. But like the world outside, unless one has more of a Calvinistic view than I have, the university is full of both saints and sinners. "Hell," Sartre wrote, "is other people." But so is Heaven. That mixture of students and teachers and subjects and passions and values may still be one means modern society has of tempering vice and even of inclining many toward virtue.

8

Teachers as Learners

*T*wenty years of work closely connected with improving college and university teaching have convinced me that how teachers learn on the job and how they continue to learn about teaching is one key to maintaining teaching excellence. The optimistic side of this conclusion is that college professors are highly capable of learning, about teaching as about anything else, that the experience of teaching makes some learning inevitable, and that institutions can both create a climate conducive to learning and foster activities that result in learning. The pessimistic side is that professors, like other human beings, tend to learn what they want to, and learning about teaching may not be among their primary wants. In addition, the divided nature of professing creates some resistance to learning about teaching and to efforts to foster such learning. Finally, institutions are neither very willing nor very ingenious in developing faculty members as teachers.

Faculty Development Efforts

I have expressed some hopes that the graduate schools would take responsibility for the development of both character and style in prospective teachers. Short of their doing that, I would settle for some sustained activities within graduate programs that gave thoughtful attention to development of ordinary teaching skills. The disciplines, themselves, as they are represented by national associations, may have done better in this respect than have individual graduate schools, though some kinds of efforts to develop teaching skills have been established in many departments. In the past twenty years, most of the major scholarly disciplines have given some attention to fostering teaching and some have mounted admirable programs — the Commission for Undergraduate Education in Biological Sciences (CUEBS) funded by the National Science Foundation, for example — or more recently, the work within economics and social sciences. Faculty development in a formal way, supported both by external and internal funds, is a modest phenomenon of the seventies. The Project to Improve College Teaching, which I directed from 1969 to 1971, had "career development of the effective college teacher" as one of its primary goals.

The history of faculty development in the past decade sheds some light on professors as learners. If one makes an analogy with industrial corporations (as universities often do in other respects), money spent for research and development of faculty is a highly justified expense. Since the "product" of higher education is an educated graduate, research and development toward improving that product are necessarily aimed at increasing the efficiency, productivity, and quality of the teaching faculty. Few universities, however, incorporate into their operating budgets funds for research and development aimed at improving instructors and instruction. The closest approximation in large research universities is the budgeted support of research, which does increase the research capabilities of the faculty. Such universities are wed to the inadequate, if not wholly mistaken, notion that supporting faculty research improves their teaching (Michalak and Friedrich, 1981; Friedrich and Michalak, 1983). Faith in a connection between faculty development and improving teaching has not yet reached a point where faculty development receives a clearly defined and substantial amount of institutional support.

The current growth of faculty development as a means of developing teaching capabilities is traceable to student protests of the late sixties about the neglect of undergraduate teaching. Some members of the faculty also felt some imbalance between the attention and money given to graduate work and research and to the undergraduate program. The public cry for accountability entered in, too, for increased efforts to evaluate teaching paralleled the growth of faculty development efforts. Finally, administrations worried about retrenchment in the seventies and alarmed about the absence of new blood coming into their institutions became receptive to the general idea of developing existing faculty.

Administrators facing pressure from faculty for development funds point out that some funds have been traditionally spent toward this end. The sabbatical leave was intended as much for renewal and development as for a reward for faithful service. Travel funds to participate in scholarly meetings can properly be called development funds. And the great number of opportunities for research support and grants available in the sixties contributed greatly to one aspect of faculty development. What is characteristic of all these is that they temporarily take faculty out of teaching and that they foster the kind of research and service that may not contribute very directly to improving teaching competence.

All this may be just as it should be. By some measures, the university's prime purpose is the advancement of knowledge. The dissemination of knowledge is a secondary purpose, and the shaping of citizens toward enhancing the quality of life may be recognized but accorded even less importance. Parent and student pressure upon the university to develop usable skills has been the most persistent countering force to this view of a university's main purpose. The emphasis upon career education, however, has its own narrow emphasis upon teaching. My point is that past commitments to faculty development have not emphasized development of teachers to the degree being emphasized in current faculty development efforts.

Like much that we know about teaching, what we know about developing faculty teaching abilities has not yet arrived at a firm set of advisable practices. Still, a great deal of experience has been gained within individual institutions and within such programs as those supported by the Lilly and Bush foundations. Most efforts are faculty-initiated programs which, in sum, indicate what faculty members think will develop teaching skills. These include seminars and workshops on teaching, leaves or released time designed to help faculty develop courses or teaching skills, funds to develop courses or strategies, funds for equipment and small grants, and provisions for campus centers to provide information and other services. In the most hard-pressed colleges, faculty members often request support for activities already supported at well-endowed institutions: travel money, leaves of any kind, small sums for instructional equipment, and the like. Faculty members in small colleges seem most receptive to faculty development efforts, perhaps because so little of that kind of support has been available and also because the closer relationships between faculty and undergraduate students probably make faculty more conscious of their primary role as teachers.

Centra (1976), attempting to measure the effectiveness of faculty development efforts, comes to a number of conclusions. The respondents at the 756 colleges and universities he surveyed thought that sizable numbers of faculty had been involved, yet "teachers who wanted to get better were the group most involved while those needing improvement were seen as least involved" (p. 59). Participation in most development activities is voluntary, Centra observes, and the means of getting wider participation are not easy to propose. "There is probably no better way to drive faculty away from a program," he writes, "than to identify it as a service for the inadequate" (p. 59). Centra's conclusions square with my own experience: all efforts to improve faculty as teachers depend on the willingness of faculty to continue learning as teachers.

Some valuable findings come out of studies of characteristics of effective teachers as perceived by faculty colleagues and students (Hildebrand and others, 1971; Wilson and others, 1975). Faculty perceived to be "especially effective or impactful. . . share a greater commitment to teaching generally; they strive to make their courses interesting; and they interact more with students and have greater rapport with them" (Wilson and others, p. 111). Though this may merely seem to confirm what anyone might have guessed, it underscores an important point: faculty members do well what they take an active interest in doing. Being interested in teaching is linked with being interested in students and in finding ways to arouse their interest.

Learning to Teach in Graduate School

It follows that if we could but interest teachers in teaching, we could expect useful learning to follow. Let us hypothesize about how college professors learn to teach and then speculate about how that learning might be fostered and prolonged within faculty development efforts.

We know that few college and university faculty members take formal course work in education as part of their programs of studies. We also know that within many faculties, there are some numbers who have taken such courses or who have given attention to teaching and learning in some specific ways. Departments of psychology have many faculty members engaged in research on learning, human development, and pedagogy; some faculty members in many departments have had previous experience as public school teachers; some eminent scholars — Jacques Barzun and Kenneth Clark are two examples — manifest a public interest in teaching. Thus, despite the fact that most Ph.D. candidates have not had formal course work or experience in how to teach, many may have experienced some development as teachers before they assume faculty positions. Most have learned about teaching in conventional ways: they have read books, have had psychology classes, have discussed teaching with knowledgeable colleagues or professors, have observed their teachers, have had some actual teaching experiences.

The matter of not having course work in pedagogy, therefore, may not be as limiting as it first appears. Formal education probably places more confidence in course work than is justified, for a tight connection between course work and specific competences in any activity is difficult to establish. As regards formal course work in education, such courses have been, fairly and unfairly, so little respected within the university's general climate that their absence from a college teacher's dossier may be no great loss.

Nevertheless, too little in the prospective college teacher's educational experience draws attention to teaching as a vital and developable skill. Among the recommendations of the various high-level committees that have studied graduate education in the past decade is one that calls for more attention to pedagogy in the graduate programs of prospective college teachers ("Newman Unit's Report on Graduate Education," 1973). In almost all graduate programs, the main emphasis is on mastery of the knowledge of a field and demonstration of research competence in some aspect of that field. These pressures squeeze out all other study and even diminish the attention a candidate might give to such an important matter as developing teaching skills. Moreover, the bias against formal "education" tends to place a barrier between subject matter departments and those engaged in education. It is a rare graduate student who can cross such a barrier to include work in pedagogy or even to seek guidance about teaching and learning.

The result is that the practical experience large numbers of graduate students receive as teaching assistants is the chief form of specific preparation for teaching. Paradoxically, Ph.D. candidates in many prestigious institutions and those whose records win them other kinds of support can escape specific preparation for teaching altogether. All candidates, it is true, experience some kind of exposure to developing their teaching skills, if only the negative kind that makes students vow not to repeat the worst of sins perpetrated by their professors. And students who remain within the formal education system from kindergarten through four or five years of graduate study must have made observations that affect their own teaching practices. But at best, the acquiring of teaching skill across the disciplines is haphazard and little informed or reinforced by the resources within the university.

The best aspect of current practices arises from employing large numbers of teaching assistants in some fields and institutions. Expediency in this respect seems to be a virtue, for assistants are customarily crammed into any available space, thus forcing an interchange about teaching not unlike the animated talk that goes on in large cocktail parties held in small rooms. Were there a wider range of experience and perspectives within such groups and a wider range of teaching situations open to the assistants, this might be the best of all possible experiences in pedagogy for future college teachers. (What the practice contributes to the unevenness of instruction for beginning undergraduates is a separate question few universities have been willing to ask.) But much is missing from this experience, and much contributes to attitudes that are inhibiting to future development. As teaching seems to have its low priority in the graduate school, so will it be given a low priority thereafter.

The pattern described varies from department to department. The employment of teaching assistants is confined to departments having large enrollments in basic courses: English, mathematics, and social sciences, for example. Research assistantships are more abundant and prized above teaching or laboratory assistantships in physics, chemistry, and engineering. Teaching assistants may have complete responsibility for a course or work as graders or readers or equipment managers. Some small part of faculty time, and usually from the lower echelons of the faculty, may be allotted to working with the assistants in various ways.

Developing Skills in Beginning Teachers

So much for what prepares professors for their first teaching jobs. When they join the faculty of a college or university, they are not likely to get much formal assistance in making the transition from graduate student to instructor. Most commonly, the new staff member is assigned a maximum number of basic courses with large numbers of students. At the same time, he or she may be finishing a dissertation or adapting the dissertation for publication or writing papers that will help establish a claim on tenure. Colleagueship will be established most strongly with other new faculty members, and professional relationships with others of the same rank assigned to the same kind of courses. This pattern is likely to remain through the five years or so it may take to achieve the kind of recognition that promises a permanent position.

There is little of formal instruction in this pattern of development, even within a milieu that could easily provide it, or even much interchange between new and experienced teachers. In this respect, American universities may be behind British ones, which in the main mandate initial training programs (albeit insubstantial ones) during a staff member's first year (Seldin, 1977). Development of teaching skills in our colleges and universities is left to the individual's inclination, self-interest, and natural aptitudes. Some forces—notably the conflicting demands placed upon the individual and the values reflected by the institution—may be against learning to teach or against valuing teaching sufficiently to learn. A great many forces are mixed. The new teacher adopts defensive strategies to keep a step ahead of the students or finds ways of shortcutting teaching to permit more time for research or adopts those practices most compatible with institutional regulations, kinds of students, and the like.

Though new teachers vary almost as widely as new students, the following generalizations might be made:

1. Even among a relatively homogeneous segment of faculty, differences in pedagogical experiences, skills, and attitudes will be great.
2. Felt pressures to teach well will be intense, but so will other pressures for establishing a secure basis for a career.
3. A feeling of being free from graduate school constraints will be replaced by some necessity to find out the real rules that pertain in this department and college and to act in conformity with them as they might affect one's future.
4. The need for practical advice about teaching will be fairly constant; the sources of such advice will chiefly be other new instructors, and even this will be less available than it was for former teaching assistants.
5. More self-consciousness will develop about teaching, because of being close to students in age, because of being removed from them by being identified as faculty, and because the new faculty occupy the lowest and most insecure faculty positions.

Past conditioning rules out highly formalized instruction in pedagogy for these new faculty members, and the conditions now pressing upon them allow little room for or receptivity toward such formalized programs. If just this diverse segment of teachers is to be taught — much more, if the aim is to affect the total faculty — learning must be informal and closely integrated with daily practice. At the same time, pressures to acquire teaching skills may be greater than a new faculty member's self-initiating capacity to meet these pressures. As the newest and most insecure group, they are not always reachable by opportunities for voluntary participation that may reveal their deficiencies, nor are they likely to take advantage of well-intentioned but vaguely defined opportunities. Facing pressures to begin producing as scholars and suspecting that the real values lie there, they are not necessarily responsive to more carefully designed but still voluntary faculty development programs, such as the holding of workshops and seminars.

This analysis of new faculty — which applies, for some other reasons, to established faculty — points to the major difficulty facing all faculty development efforts: getting the faculty most in need of development to participate. The gap between what is available and what is put to use should bedevil teachers and administrators even more than it does. The gap is notable with respect to students' taking advantage of the

rich resources a university affords. It is a fundamental obligation of
faculty, too little recognized by most, to increase the willingness of students to use what is there. Appreciation for a wider learning runs into a
conflict with the learning close at hand; the narrow teacher keeps the student bent to his or her narrow range of demands and squeezes out much
that might be more valuable. Similarly, the work of administrators
might well include the obligation to raise the possibility that faculty take
advantage of the rich resources that a university affords. In particular,
department and division heads or chairpersons have the inescapable
obligation of getting faculty to take advantage of the resources that are
available to develop teaching skill. Without such persuasive and coercive
forces within a university, faculty development efforts are bound to get
an insufficient response.

A recent empirical study (Fink, 1982) of 100 beginning teachers
in their first year as faculty members in geography departments confirms
the generalizations just made. The fact that about half of the new
appointments in the 1976–1978 period were in nontenure track positions
emphasizes the high degree of insecurity among beginning faculty members today. Almost all of these teachers had had experience as teaching
assistants and regarded that experience as valuable. A good number had
taken education courses, but the majority had low opinions of their
worth. Only one third had completed their dissertations before starting
in these full-time positions; one third finished during the first year.
Working on the dissertation was a major conflict with teaching, since a
majority had four to eight different preparations in their first year and
about three fourths felt they had an excessive teaching load. About two
thirds of these teachers found themselves in institutions somewhat or
very different from the kind they identified with as students, and about
the same number noted a lack of "intellectual companionship" with their
new colleagues. Both affected their teaching performances adversely. As
to their actual teaching, most tended to adopt the most conventional lecture form. The quality of their work varied widely from class to class;
about two thirds were judged to be performing adequately or better.
About the same number said they experienced "psychic satisfactions"
from the year's work, though as many as one third expressed feelings of
frustration and disillusionment. Neither the graduate school nor the
institution they joined as faculty did a great deal to develop teaching
skills or give any but routine support to their teaching.

Chairpersons as Faculty Developers

If this sampling is fairly representative, the inducting of college teachers into the profession is hardly better than the inducting of freshmen into large universities. Administrations are as much to blame as faculty. No one person in the academic community is closer to the functioning of faculty as teachers than the department or division chair. No one should be more skillfully responsive to their needs. For one faculty member, it may be a succession of visits to classes and thoughtful exchange after. For others, it may be initiating a monthly discussion group in which a new faculty member is made to feel at home. For still others, it may be an invitational workshop with colleagues from within and outside one's field. Some actions may be mandatory; a chairperson is as responsible for seeing that a group of faculty carry out the aims of a many-sectioned course as for seeing that individual classes are staffed and met. Some actions may be only indirectly coercive; the chairperson makes clear that such and such an activity is specifically for developing teachers and it is in the interest of faculty to attend. Some may be as voluntary as the kind of social gatherings that invite by their attractiveness rather than by advantages to be gained or lost in attending.

In another crucial way, the chairperson is central. He or she is responsible for making clear to faculty members what the real rules and values of the department are. More, the chairperson is the only figure who, with a faculty's backing, can resist an institution's tendency to give lip service to teaching. The interest the chairperson takes in a new faculty member's teaching is but the other side of a tangible advocacy of teaching that makes it possible for new faculty members to develop as teachers without jeopardizing their careers.

Finally, it is the chairperson who can, by management of committees, teaching assignments, office assignments, and social gatherings, resist the tendency toward age and rank groupings and bring about exchange among all faculty which can favorably affect a teacher's work. As so much of learning about teaching is personal, experiential, even anecdotal, so teaching may be best affected by establishing department dynamics that foster exchange across conventional lines. The young can learn from the old, and the old from the young, but only if the inclinations and habits and stereotypes are confronted that make it difficult for young and old to have an easy and productive interchange. The kind of activities, formal and informal, mandatory and voluntary, that bring together young and old, specialists of one kind and specialists of another, researchers and teachers, can best be initiated and carried out by a department chairperson, though that does not mean a proprietary right over such activities or preclude the involvement of other faculty.

These suggestions for the expanded role of chairpersons are made with full recognition that college administrators are probably more poorly prepared for their positions than are college teachers. Upper-level positions benefit from the experience acquired at the lower levels, but department chairs and division heads customarily lack specific preparation, get little or no on-the-job training, operate under vaguely defined and shifting responsibilities, and carry out vitally important functions amidst much faculty misunderstanding and even disrespect. Suffice to say here that however much faculty may be engaged in planning and supervising their own development as teachers, effective faculty development depends heavily on the daily functioning of department and division chairs and on the support provided them by higher administrators.

Teaching Awards and Other Incentives

Close-at-hand encouragement and stimulation, and when necessary, even coercion and correction, are more effective in the continuing learning of college teachers than institutional pressures. Nevertheless, even a president of a large university can affect teaching, if not personally, then in the responsibilities he or she places upon other administrators all down the line. Seeing that administrators value teaching, are active in specific support and development of teaching, and work effectively within designated faculty development programs is probably more important than specific actions a president might take. Teaching awards, for example, are a limited resource for giving tangible recognition to teaching, one of the least effective practices for faculty development according to Centra (1976, pp. 62–63). Usually they are identified with the institution at large, and more for public relations purposes than for improving teaching. About as many commonplace mistakes are made in the handling of teaching awards as in any other aspect of university administration. Given the size and diversity of an institution and the inadequacy of the procedures for identifying "best teachers," single awards for teacher of the year are as much fomenters of discord as stimuli to good teaching. Multiple awards and a rotating of awards among the colleges or departments are better practices. Making something of the expertise of those who have received such awards should also be a common practice; a cadre of teachers recognized as outstanding could provide a central resource for any faculty development program.

But teaching awards may not be a very good way of indicating institutional support; they often exist because other ways are lacking. Internal grants that provide tangible support — not rewards — for good teaching are probably a better way of spending money. And even beyond such tangible efforts, the creation of an administrative structure composed of persons who know about teaching, value it, are ingenious in finding ways to support it, and who are shrewd developers of teachers is a much more necessary achievement for a president or academic vice-president who wants to make an impact.

Somewhat as we place our faith and money in educating our citizens when they are young, so the main stress in faculty development might well be on development in the graduate schools and in the early years of service as faculty members. But, there is still room for and need for keeping learning opportunities open for faculty members throughout their careers. Good teachers do continue to learn. And mediocre teachers may include those who have never learned, never developed, as well as those who have lost along the way an interest in teaching which fosters continuing learning. Here, again, the wise administering of department and division chairs is vital, not only to affect individual faculty members, whatever their condition, but to provoke and sustain a department's general interest in teaching. Achieving that, such an administrator may not have to intervene personally with a teacher who has slipped below the minimal standards a university wants to maintain. Teachers who have become plodders may have become so in part because of the absence of a milieu in which teaching matters, in which it is easy to share one's ideas and enthusiasms and failings with others, in which recognition is generously accorded, and in which changes that affect a person's teaching through a career are both respected and put to good use.

It is commonly argued that change is the most important stimulation to making the most of a person's middle years. For some teachers, achievements bring opportunities for stimulating change; for others, their own energies and initiative make them thrust out in new directions. The professor of middling competence may not be able to count on either.

No wonder, one might reflect, that research careers seem to offer greater attractions than teaching. Through achievements in specialized research, a professor gains an invitation to an international conference or to fill a visiting appointment at another university. But few are the opportunities for beneficent change for those who have gained local acclaim as teachers.

It follows that enlargement of opportunities for faculty members to experience changes favorable to teaching would be worth money spent. A domestic Fulbright program, particularly in view of the gaps, not only in quality but also in values and perceptions, between our small and large universities, might do as much good as the international Fulbright exchange. Not having that, more institutions could facilitate faculty exchange within similar institutions. Even changes in teaching assignments that might have to be skillfully coerced by a department chair can be a source of revitalization. And though talk is cheap and faculties get easily surfeited by it, more opportunities might be created to get faculty together for an afternoon or weekend to engage in discourse on teaching, not as a task assignment for some specific end but as a pleasant excuse to step back from day-to-day teaching and reflect on teaching in the large.

The tendency to equate deadwood on a faculty with the aged and long-tenured is probably impossible to counter. Worse perhaps, and much less observed, is that excellence in teaching is not associated with the acquiring of wisdom that might be associated with age. The youth-consciousness of American culture is inescapable in a university where the main student body perpetually stays in its twenties. Both tendencies must be opposed if college teachers are to remain effective in their later years, extended now by the ending of mandatory retirement. Deadwood is probably fairly widely distributed among ranks, though it must be acknowledged that some culling takes place through the years. Declining vigor and the infirmities of aging may well deplete the necessary energy that helps give teaching distinction. In other ways, too, old faculty members wear out, the students too much the same or worse, the faculty mired in its routine, the institution disappointing in what it once promised, the battles over educational principles fought and refought to no clear ends.

Ministering to the senior ranks of teachers must acknowledge all of these possibilities. Not much can be done about some entrenched mediocrity, nor can vigor and health be prolonged or restored in specific instances. But something might be done to shift both attitudes and assignments in later years and to the benefit of all. I have in mind vigorous efforts to tap some totality of experience of senior professors, rather than continuing to draw on depleted resources of specialized competence.

As one way of proceeding, much more could be made of "university professors," a designation largely honorary now but which could be opened up for those who, as they are true university citizens, have more to offer than mere department affiliation allows. Such a rank would not include everyone as a right of age but it might include a good many who had earned the rank and others who would move in those directions because of the rank. Provided with another identification than attachment to a department, university professors might take on a common identity distinguished by a broader and deeper conception of the aims of education. They might even function as a council of elders among whose prerogatives and privileges would be that of introducing into the curriculum courses that did not fit the tidiness of majors and minors and electives. They would not fit, either, the tidy conception of courses for students and not for faculty. Some part of the university professor's efforts could well be channeled into teaching the faculty.

Such broadening of opportunities, recognizing of changing interests and perspectives, is indicated for making more of the teaching capacities of some professors. Those who continue to be productive researchers and writers have their own sources of renewal, though even among the very productive there are those who choose new emphases and directions. The highest excellence probably makes its own way, though that way as regards university faculties may not necessarily serve the teaching interests of the university.

Often, it is just such wresting out of context that gives a senior professor new teaching life. It is commonly the young professors, newly arrived from graduate school, fresh with the latest research and still conversant with the undergraduates they were a few years ago, who gain the fevered response of multitudes of students. Those same professors grown older may well find that they have been superseded by the "smarts" of younger faculty. Reaching sixty, they may even experience some jealousies toward the young colleagues who turn students on. Being wiser as well as older and still vitally interested in teaching, they may find it challenging to draw upon their own strengths to maintain an impact upon students. Some things will be easier: they can be less con-

cerned with being on top of or up to date on or even "on" every day; they
can be more honest and forthright, more tolerant and merciful without
implying a disrespect for discipline and rigor. Other things will be
harder: speaking the students' language, for example, or even being conversant with it; resisting a tendency to think everything has been tried;
overcoming the distances that separate incoming students and retiring
faculty; and resisting the ease of slipping into comfortable routines that
will get one safely to retirement.

Being little inclined to change with the times and being irritated,
moreover, with being old, a professor may need a change of context.
Many university professors have found that change in a gradual movement from undergraduate to graduate courses and students. Their
teaching may be no better, or worse, but the students' forced tolerance is
greater and the number adversely affected fewer. But great numbers of
colleges offer no such opportunities for that kind of change. For those
colleges and professors, other efforts must be made to help aging professors find new contexts.

Limitations of Faculty Development Efforts

In all that I have said about teachers as learners, I have put much
emphasis upon professors being taught to teach or, at least, being opened
up to influences that would promote learning. It would seem reasonable
enough that those who make their living by teaching might be responsive
to being taught. Alas, I fear it is not so. Most people resist being taught
what they already think they know. Professors resist strongly, and usually
in proportion to the felt pressure being applied from the outside. Conse-
quently, all faculty development efforts are low key, the need minimized,
the availability of help not greatly advertised, and participation strictly a
matter of the faculty member's own choosing. The model is clearly the
psychiatric one; the patient must acknowledge a need for treatment if the
treatment is to be effective. A mental health model, however, in which the
availability of help is emphasized and the stigma and difficulties of seeking it out are reduced is at least as appropriate. Faculty development
efforts would be directed toward raising the level of acceptance of doing
something about gaining such skills. Academic institutions may be
caught in a split in their own educational practices. One strong bias
among a faculty is that they and their college or university are there to be

sought out by those who wish to learn. The selective practices of prestige colleges and the concept of a research institution devoid of students support this view. The other bent is that of continuing education and extension services: the college brings its wares to an audience, drops its presumptions about who can benefit, and lives by creating new students and a wider desire to learn.

Faculty development that is low key and purely voluntary cannot meet the needs of this wider view of higher education's services, if those needs are taken seriously. If teachers are to continue learning as teachers, there must be inescapable reinforcement of teaching, opportunities to develop in these directions, and rewards that attach to participation.

There are opportunities here that have barely been tapped, for teaching is an essentially engaging activity. If that living character is not deadened by bad teaching, faculty development has a change to succeed. By bad teaching, I mean much the same as one easily finds in college and university classrooms: too much talking to and not enough talking with; too much asserting of authority and not of intelligence and compassion; too much theorizing and not enough enlightened practice; too much that is compromised by the need to fit packaging and grading and teaching requirements. No faculty development will succeed that merely relies on encouraging ordinary professors to teach in ordinary ways. Many — the majority of professors, I would argue — have higher personal expectations than that, and if their expectations are to be met, they, like other students, will be responsive to learning.

Student and Other Evaluations of Teaching

A word need be said about student evaluation and other means of ascertaining teaching competence. Like the grading of students, the evaluating of teachers may or may not assist in improving an individual teacher's learning. However, the same faculty that may accept grades as tightly related to students' learning may resist the notion that student evaluations are important to their own learning. To be sure, there are differences in grades and student evaluations, but the main difference may be in who is being graded.

Faculty development is hard to separate from the evaluating of teachers, for identifying ineffective teachers, by whatever measures, seems to argue that means should be provided to develop competence.

If student evaluations can be viewed neutrally — and that may require separating them from promotion, tenure, and salary discussions — they can provide very useful specific diagnostic information. Their use by an increasing number of institutions suggests a higher degree of acceptance than in the past. Seldin's survey for 1981–82 shows that nearly 70 percent of the colleges reported using student evaluations as a major source of information about teaching — up from about 35 percent ten years ago (Seldin, 1983, p. 155). Impressive as these figures are, they may only indirectly indicate faculty acceptance; the increase must be in part charged to the obvious utility for both faculty and administrators of student evaluations in making promotion, tenure, and salary decisions.

Though many questions have been answered among those commonly raised about student evaluations, two important ones have not been and are not likely to be answered precisely. The first is whether student evaluations actually improve a faculty member's teaching, and the second is whether the more effective teacher as measured by student evaluation actually improves the students' learning. The problems of setting up a research design that might answer either question are staggering. What anecdotal and common-sense evidence we have suggests that student evaluations — any consistent and accepted increased interest in the particulars of teaching — do help teachers develop skills. If we believe that teaching is important to students' learning, then more effective teaching — again, by almost any reasonable measure — may improve the students' learning.

The case for student evaluations really rests there. They do provide one means by which faculty are better able to judge how they are engaging the attention of all students in a class, and engaging attention is basic to learning. They also have the effect of drawing teachers' attention to the particulars of their teaching, again basic to performing any skill well. Beyond that, they may affect the reward system so that teaching can have more weight in advancement and salary decisions. And, they may be linked with faculty development efforts whereby faculty assist other faculty to develop identified skills.

I will make no attempt to discuss the wrangling that still breaks out over student evaluations. The literature by now is copious and open to all faculty members willing to be guided by what they might learn rather than by what they already think they know. Some of the important and current sources are Centra (1979), Costin (1971), French-

Lazovik (1982), Kulik and McKeachie (1975), McKeachie (1979), and Overall and Marsh (1982).

Student evaluations have obvious practical advantages over other means by which teaching may be evaluated. Foremost, they cost the faculty less of their own time than do any measures that rely on classroom visits of faculty by faculty or on any close scrutiny by faculty of what makes up a teacher's skill. As a judgment of classroom performance, student evaluations are better than faculty visits because the basis of judgment takes in all students, all classes, and attendant factors that relate to the students' perceptions of learning in ways that no sample visits by faculty can. The practical considerations do not mean that faculty should not be involved in trying to assess teaching in additional ways. But faculty members interested in learning about their teaching cut off a vital source of information if, for whatever reasons, they are hostile or indifferent to student evaluations.

Gaining Insight into Learning

Finally, a consideration of how professors learn to teach can be greatly informed by reflecting on what and how professors continue to learn about other things. The writing of a book is one way, for it may well force the professor into mastering at least an elementary knowledge of many disciplines. Like the sculptor who must learn to be a welder or metallurgist or master mason or geologist, professors who attempt a large understanding of a complex subject may have to acquire many skills. Similarly, a great deal of disparate learning takes place as a result of the demands teaching places upon teachers. And, as should be appropriate for professors, almost all of this learning is self-learning arising from need and answered by turning to the resources that a university supplies.

Very little of the university's *human* teaching resources are drawn upon in this kind of faculty learning. Most colleges and universities place no barriers against professors' attending classes; few professors do. Were they more willing to place themselves in the actual position of students as learners in formal classes, many professors might gain useful insight into the mysteries of teaching and learning as well.

I will be personal and anecdotal here. I have been trying to learn French for some thirty years now, off and on, after having learned enough reading French to pass a Ph.D. exam. My classroom work was entirely toward reading comprehension, a mistake common to language instruction in the past. The efficiency of short-term results won out over a longer view in which language is ill served by such dismembering. Left with no ability to understand or speak French, I periodically tried to take oral French classes, usually in the evening and always unsuccessfully. As an assistant professor, insecure enough in other ways, the humiliation of reciting and bumbling was such that I usually dropped the class within a few weeks. My official excuses, like those of other students, were that I was too busy with more important matters and that I would do it later when I had more time.

Later kept arriving and being put off until still later. The last two experiences were ones I persisted in for a number of months each, and though I did not learn much spoken French, I did learn many interesting things about learning. In the first of these, I had the good fortune to have as a teacher a graduate student just back from an exciting year in France. Despite her nonthreatening presence and endless encouragement and support, I still found my inhibitions almost as strong as before. I continued to engage in dodges familiar to all students: I prayed I would not be called on, hid my responses when I could among the group's responses, found good excuses not to attend classes at all when I had had no time to prepare. The classes were not a complete loss, but they did not overcome my learning disabilities.

The second experience was an experimental course suggested to me by a colleague in the French department who had been trying the method on advanced students. The only thing advanced about me was my age, though I did have a rudimentary knowledge of French grammar and syntax and a modest French vocabulary—not, it need be said, of words as they are spoken but as they appear on the written page, two quite different things. The method had at its center a video tape of the movie *La Symphonie Pastorale*. With minimum involvement of the teacher, the student was left free to play and replay the tape of the movie and acquire in context an ability to understand and to speak. I exposed myself to the tape several hours a day, at first with a colleague who gave up before he ever found out what happened to the blind girl and the too sympathetic pastor. At our request, we were furnished with a written script in French, which greatly aided me in comprehending what was happening. At the end of several months, I think I might have been able to recognize phrases of a living French man and woman caught in the same situation as the erring priest and the blind girl and speaking exactly the same lines. What I did learn with some sense of conviction was that, for the first time, I understood how spoken French was put together and that one might go about learning to understand and even to speak it. To take the next step, I concluded, a living teacher, as accessible as a video recorder, would have been a necessity. And probably more than a teacher, a whole context of my having to learn and finding no way to escape.

Out of both experiences, I learned little French, but I did learn or had reinforced some important aspects of learning. First, I learned how much my students' learning is inhibited by their not wanting to make mistakes, dodging what is difficult for them, following the paths of other interests or less resistant learning. Even now, I am talking about learning from this experience — not the speaking of French, which is foreign and difficult, but the learning of something about teaching, which is congenial and comfortable. Second, I was forced to ponder again the relationship between present learning and new learning. The matter is complex. I think my own knowledge of reading French both helped and got in the way of a seemingly closely related learning. Perhaps the learning is not that closely related, the distance between ear and eye being much greater than the physical distance on one's face. It was at times almost as if I were a dog whose whole world was through the nose being asked to comprehend everything through the printed page. Third, I had to revive my past respect for exceptional language teachers I have had and increase my respect for Professor John Rassias, whose teaching of French has made him a national figure (Wolkomir, 1980). My classroom experiences verify the essential rightness of his method. Inhibitions to language learning are indeed so great that only great effort can overpower them. With Professor Rassias, much of this effort is physical, purposeful battering to release the hold that our self-protecting mental apparatuses have upon us. The standard method of encouraging response, of even forcing response in polite ways, is of little use with students like myself.

My young French teacher had not yet acquired the repertoire of conning and cajoling and threatening and bullying and deceiving and dramatizing that is primarily aimed at surmounting the resistance after which learning can take place. And yet, make no mistake about it. The teacher must project a presence that does not drive a student away. As much as I admire French, find myself comfortable and energized at the same time while I am in France, abstractly want to learn to speak French, the actual *doing* of it, without reinforcement in the living world that surrounds me, falls short for want of the sustained effort that goes into a complex and often laborious learning. That, it seems to me, is the position of a majority of subjects college professors teach to the majority of students who confront them. Our work as teachers cannot count on the vitality of the subject itself nor the impulses of the student to learn nor a reinforcing context in the culture. We must provide assistance both to overcome the students' own internal impediments to learning and to increase the willingness of the student to work at this particular kind of learning.

In sum, professors learn pretty much as anyone else does. Those who came into teaching because it was the most compelling interest they had probably learned early and continued to learn how to teach well. Those who did not come to teaching by that route probably entertain some idea of doing better, if they find out that they are not doing very well somewhere along the way, but the ways of doing better must overcome resistances and find encouragement. Teaching teachers to teach or even to learn about teaching may not be the best way of approaching the creation of better teachers. From the outside, insofar as the outside can do anything to affect internal motivation, creating a climate in which teaching is a vibrant, satisfying, and ponderable activity may be the basic condition. Within such a climate, too, gifted individuals highly committed to teaching might more visibly and effectively function as teachers of other teachers.

9

Teaching's Highest Aims

Alfred North Whitehead's *The Aims of Education*, first published in 1929, is a collection of essays and papers delivered to various audiences from 1912 to 1928. "One main idea runs through the various chapters," Whitehead wrote. "The students are alive, and the purpose of education is to stimulate and guide their self-development" (1949 [1929], p. ix). The book is wise and perceptive, and unusual because a philosopher of the first rank addresses himself to education and specifically in several essays to teachers in the lower schools. The distance between professional philosophy and education, between university professors and public school teaching, between professors pursuing their disciplines and teachers teaching has widened during the twentieth century. A partial explanation is that all disciplines have become more distant from one another as they have increased in size and in the scope and complexity of their subject matters. As the expectations for advanced education have grown, so have the numbers of college and university professors, creating difficulties in maintaining identity across subject matters, much more across the array of separate courses that define teaching. The difficulty of the American Association of University Professors (AAUP) in maintaining membership, evident for at least a decade, speaks to this condition. Membership in AAUP is an acknowledgment of the common tasks and aims of university professors regardless of their disciplinary affiliations. For an increasing number of professors today, the sense of common purpose is not very strong.

Whitehead is only one of a number of remarkable philosopher-teachers in our history. Within the present, the profiles of great teachers collected by Joseph Epstein in *Masters: Portraits of Great Teachers* include many men and women of this kind, and his selections by no means include all those who could be similarly recognized. Bertrand Russell, Whitehead's most illustrious pupil and collaborator, described him as "extraordinarily perfect as a teacher. He took a personal interest in those with whom he had to deal and knew both their strong and their weak points. He would elicit from a pupil the best of which a pupil was capable. He was never repressive, or sarcastic, or superior or any of the things that inferior teachers like to be. I think that in all the abler young men with whom he came in contact he inspired, as he did in me, a very real and lasting affection" (Epstein, 1981, p. 61). What might most be acquired from these extraordinary teachers is a belief both in learning — without such a belief all other optimistic prospects recede from sight — and in teaching that embraces ends as higher than techniques.

Despite some disillusionment in the immediate present, our time sets much store by higher education. The commitment reveals itself in a steady increase in this century of the numbers attending colleges and universities and of the average years of formal schooling in the populace, in the rising percentage of students going on to college and university, and in the numbers of institutions of higher education. Such an expanding phenomenon surely must have some driving motivations beyond those furnished by an increasing population.

Traditional Aims of American Higher Education

Traditionally, these motivations — aims of American higher education, if you will — are: (1) the development of a highly educated citizenry as basic to a complex and functioning democracy; (2) the expansion of knowledge for such practical ends as improving crops, roads, health, and so on, and the training of professionals to carry out these practical ends both through research and practice; and (3) the fostering of the arts, sciences, and humanities as contributing to the creation of an attractive culture. Most of the activities and achievements of American colleges and universities can be placed within these categories, as can most of the activities and achievements of individual professors. It should be added that those many colleges founded by religious sects directly embraced moral aims, emphasizing (4) a tie between education and moral and ethical development that is acknowledged by most institutions even if it may be in the form of a more fully developed and realized self.

These four categories provide a framework for the discussion of the aims of college and university teachers. Acceptable as I think they are to most teachers in the abstract, they need translating into goals that define the transactions and chores that constitute teaching. Attempting to set them forth is no erecting of standards of practice; they serve rather as a set of reminders to all teachers, regardless of discipline and of the immediate task at hand, that larger aims should inform their practices.

Toward Civic Responsibility

Let us begin with the shaping of citizens for a democracy. To a large degree, it is the willingness of the self to accommodate to the needs of others that distinguishes an effective political democracy. Justification of the priority of the self over others inclines one to the sins previously discussed — to arrogance, vanity, self-indulgence, insensitivity, and rigidity, if not to hypocrisy and dullness. A Carnegie Foundation report by Boyer and Hechinger (Scully, 1981) makes the case for civic learning clearly: "Unless we find better ways to educate ourselves *as citizens*, we run the risk of drifting unwittingly into a new kind of Dark Ages — a time when small cadres of specialists will control knowledge and thus control the decision-making process" (p. 1). Like the argument I am making here, theirs is also based on a fundamental premise of democracy: "This nation began with a conviction, at once deceptively simple and profound, that for democracy to work, education is essential" (p. 12).

The political aims of American education are both simple and complex. Were education not embedded in and supported by a democ-

racy, it could indulge its seemingly natural bent toward privilege, exclusiveness, and singularity. The European models we inherited were
basically aristocratic models: higher education reserved for the upper
classes and allied with training of a ruling elite. American education has
long been involved crucially in the central democratic paradox: a culture
that preaches equality and yet provides means and incentives to become
unequal as quickly as possible. The history of American education could
be adequately described in terms of accommodations to this paradox.
On the one hand, public schooling has steadily been extended to the
entire populace and for an increased number of years. On the other, the
upper reaches of that education are the access routes to privileged positions in society and have become increasingly specialized.

One could argue that the two movements are part of the same
democratic extension of education. The widening at the lower end
inevitably leads to widening at the upper. More of the democratic mix of
population will find their way into the graduate schools. In time, every
political candidate, if not every voter, will have advanced degrees, and a
harmony will have been effected between an aristocracy of intellect,
loosely defined, and a democratically governed polity.

In the meantime, higher education is at the center of more complex political aims. In the large, higher education, despite its depen-
dence on broad-based public support, has been granted a large measure
of aristocratic privilege. One of the largely unrecognized difficulties
facing lower public schooling is that it is thus marked off from higher
education. Public school superintendents and principals have become
increasingly less educators and more public officials, their numbers coming from training in educational administration or from experience at
the greatest point of public exposure as athletic coaches. Public pressure
on the schools is direct and consequential. They are necessarily democratic institutions, faced with granting equal status to all students, forced
attendance through mid-adolescence, and only the possibility of internal
differentiations to serve differences in student aptitudes. That equality of
status and treatment of racial minorities is still short of reality does not
alter the prevailing democratic ideal and practices.

Higher education has been drawn ever closer to these facts of
public lower schooling. The professors' complaints that their college or
university is becoming "just a glorified high school" are surprising only
in that any other course might have been expected. The lines between

undergraduate colleges and graduate schools today may roughly approximate that between public high schools and colleges early in the century. As a matter of course, then, undergraduate higher education has been drawn into educating for citizenship, whether through American institutions, courses mandated by legislatures or through general education programs that have exposure to the political and social sciences as an important component. Nor is it surprising that, at the same time, graduate schools have retreated further into specialization and preoccupation with subject matters.

Marking off and defining areas where differences can flourish is an obvious democratic accommodation, perhaps an inescapable fact of growth and sophistication. As public lower schooling is wholly concerned with mass education, higher education even at the undergraduate level is permitted to retain some of its notions related to education for the few. At the same time, however, the extension of public education to include much postsecondary schooling creates inescapable pressures on most colleges and universities toward mass education.

If this brief analysis squares with the important facts, what does it say to the college and university teacher about teaching that would be wisely cognizant of democratic political aims? First, I think it says that the vast majority of college professors are in the business of public schooling. They must accept the fact and work to further it along the best lines rather than fight to preserve a special status that cannot be preserved. That entails accepting the kind of students they face—a cross section of the populace—rather than fussing about the kinds of students who should be there. It entails sustaining and developing strong general education rather than fighting to get back to or arrive at specialized education at odds with both public needs and support. It entails looking more respectfully at civic aims in education rather than rejecting the political as an encroachment of the state or an intrusion of secondary instrumental concerns into the primary abstract intellectual ones.

As to teaching itself, acceptance of the political dimensions of education would not result in such marked separations of citizens from teachers as have been true in the past. We have inherited suspicions from the past as well as inclinations of the present that separate church and state, politics and education, home and work, family and profession. And yet, as the success of a democratic polity has broken down many of the discriminatory aspects of race and sex, so might these other separations be rendered less harmful. A teacher does not have to endorse school prayer to assert the presence of spirituality as a dimension of human life. Nor do teachers have to promulgate the platforms of Democrats or Republicans or Libertarians to assert the importance of students' embracing civic responsibilities. As I began this book by emphasizing style and character, so I here emphasize the importance of citizenship as an integral part of a teacher's presence and aims.

Academic liberals and conservatives alike have been prone to suspect that any stressing of civic responsibility is a covert attempt to intrude the ideologies they oppose. The detachment necessary to scholarship has added weight to the argument that withdrawal from political concerns is the only safe course for a college or university teacher. Detachment has not necessarily proved to be a safe course in those egregious instances where the state has imposed an ideology, nor has withdrawal contributed to the stemming of ideologies that proved barbarous. The difficulty seems to be that of developing civic responsibility without inculcating an ideology. Facing that difficulty begins with recognizing that the development of civic responsibility is a high and legitimate aim of higher education. If we succeed as teachers, we should expect our students to take on the duties of citizens — to use the qualities of mind, the access to knowledge and acquisition of skills, the breadth of outlook, resistance to dogma, and compassion for others that our teaching has embraced, in behalf of the public weal.

Few teachers would object to these general aims; they might, however, fight against specific courses aimed to improve economic or political literacy. The drift of this book is that general aims are best achieved by the indirect and collective impact of individual teachers functioning in light of these aims rather than by the direct and specific impact of mandated course work. However, the aim of a more enlightened and responsible carrying out of civic responsibilities is importantly qualified by the endorsement of democracy as the political framework for that aim. If we accept that qualification, teaching must necessarily be democratic, or at the least, not negate, in attitude and act, democratic ideals.

Here a teacher faces both personal and institutional conflicts. Equality of teacher and student, like equal access and opportunity, is, at best, another democratic fiction. Even those who accept the fiction know that the truth of simple facts cannot be established by majority vote nor can the understanding of complex relationships be a mere matter of consensus agreement. The one who knows, clearly the teacher within a subject matter, is superior in these respects, and any departure from that recognition threatens the learning of those who do not know.

Were teaching and learning as simple as these pronouncements, the principles of pedagogy could be mastered in a day. As they are not, the teacher must begin by acknowledging steadily if not obsessively the internal strains that do and should exist between teachers and students raised in a democracy. These are independent of subject matter, as important to acknowledge in a class in thermodynamics as in one in American institutions. As regards teachers, such an acknowledgment means a deliberate giving up of some of their authority in favor of respecting the students' authority in such matters as asking questions without fear of reprisal, voicing opinions even when fact seems most to apply, and bringing to bear what they may know or have experienced on the subject matter at hand. Relinquishing authority has other consequences: it encourages active involvement and participation; it enlarges a respect for judgment and consensus; it emphasizes that actions must often proceed where neither authority nor exact knowledge can provide the way. In short, it allows freedom the play it must have if either learning or democracy is to flourish.

In addition, teachers mindful of democratic responsibilities would modify the prevailing individualistic competitive model for learning by embracing more of cooperation and group effort. The classroom would become a paradigm of how individual excellence can be put back into the service of the body politic. A report prepared by a class on actual conditions in a single public school could be as illuminating to a community as the overview gathered together by a national commission. Finding out about the dimensions of child abuse or difficulties faced by the handicapped or the extent of environmental damage of many kinds could be a first step to linking actuality with theory and book learning, again as a means of arriving at a group report that might indeed affect those to whom it was addressed. The overriding concerns of peace and war, sources of energy, historical and environmental preservation—the list is long and varied—could provide a purposeful focus for the work of intelligent citizens who happen to be college students gathered togeth' in classes in which collective experience and intelligence is often slight in favor of individually fostered achievement.

I am not saying examples of this kind are not to be found, rather that their numbers are too few considering the great numbers of classes students take and the relevance of many of these classes to the world we live in. Some will argue that college and university study should foster the contemplative mind, give the student opportunity to theorize and explore somewhat removed from the pressures of application. I have no quarrel with such a view except as it argues for a purity that never has existed or is likely to exist. Contemplation can be shared as well as private activity. Nor am I wedded to group processes as necessarily superior to individual study. What I am asking for is some consequential breaking away from the individualistic competitive model of learning in which the individual grade for an individual course looms largest in both the student's and the faculty member's minds. Individually measured accomplishments are but one measure; achievements of class can be intentionally affirmed, and those achievements measured against even broader goals. The teacher needs to be dislodged as the only point of learning, and grades dislodged as the only measure of accomplishment. The goal is to establish in some important parts of the college years that working together can be as productive, as satisfying, and as necessary as working alone.

Such teaching as I am advocating, "democratic teaching," to use a phrase that will irritate many professors, is not being urged on ideological grounds. Clearly, democracy is an ideology, and as we value it, it can properly stand as one of the aims of education, the question of its absolute value aside. But the aim here is consistent with very high aims of learning itself. The means advocated are also consistent, if we are aiming at the development of an individual's capacities to learn independently and the enlargement of receptivity to all the many ways learning can be accomplished. And as our ideals for learning go beyond individual development, either because we cannot confine learning to its individual consequence or because individuals must live together, so we can favor a kind of learning that deliberately embraces social responsibility.

As is clear from arguments elsewhere in the text, the need for education to see itself in the light of human survival is something new in recent human history. Perhaps it only existed, previously, at a much less complicated level, when education was confined to the necessary skills by which hunters and pastoral tribes secured food and protected themselves from their enemies. If I link education with citizenship and more precisely with democracy, it is because I see survival not in terms of a strong American democracy winning out over Russian totalitarianism, but in terms of what major forces in the world animated by democratic sentiments can do to curb the world-destroying powers at their disposal. Put in other terms, we must learn to survive as successful social beings, not just as successful individuals marking off our learning in quantitative specialized accomplishments or as tribal members separating ourselves from other tribes by the marks of race and geography and past history.

I disagree at this point with Whitehead. From the vantage of the 1980s, I think he might have chastened the rhetoric of a half century earlier: "In the condition of modern life the rule is absolute, the race which does not value trained intelligence is doomed" (p. 26). We may be doomed, whether we value trained intelligence or not, and ironically doomed by the very trained intelligence we value. If we cannot bring more of that intelligence to bear upon social survival and even against the insistent urgings of self, education is a prime agent in that doom.

Teaching Toward Practical Ends

The three other broad aims of teaching are easier to discuss. We are more accustomed to perceiving teaching in relation to practical ends and to improving the quality of life, and there are strong currents connecting higher education to self-development and moral and ethical ends. I will no more than acknowledge teaching and its relation to practical ends. We have been enormously successful here, and students continue to vex some professors because they respond to that success. They come to college because they see it as an avenue to interesting, profitable, and satisfying careers, but the professor may see it as having a value in itself. The difficulty is to keep from letting teaching as transmission of information and development of skills stand for all that teaching entails. Frequent complaints from former students about not having learned anything in college that was useful on the job probably do point to the superior attraction that theory has for college professors and to their limited acquaintance with nonacademic careers. Only a handful of universities in most of their programs make strong connections between work and programs of study. Only the community colleges — at the low end of the pecking order — have large numbers of teachers who maintain close ties between schooling and jobs. (I am not speaking here of preparation for academic positions or for the professions, where such connections are maintained.) I would like to see more colleges and universities foster faculty development that expanded the number of faculty privileged to go back and forth between teaching and study and its practical applications: political scientists to run for political office — and sometimes to win; historians to serve local, state, and national historical agencies; English professors to be employed as writers of various kinds.

Focusing directly on the classroom, I would like to see teachers make active doing other than lecturing as much a part of their daily activities as possible. Even the most textbook-bound subject has some connection with doing, whether it be in the physical phenomena it explains or the drama inherent in history and literature. By both bringing into the classroom and taking the students out, teachers have great opportunities to provide real contexts for abstract studies. In these and other ways, the teacher can represent more evenhandedly the relationships between thinking and doing than the students' experience may have afforded. Working with the mind is not doing nothing. Wanting to find useful work by attending college is not a small or unworthy aim. Finding useful and satisfying work that draws upon skills, attitudes, and knowledge acquired in college is a good return for both the teacher's and student's investment.

Teaching Toward Cultural Ends

The third of these broad aims of higher education is the fostering of those studies that directly contribute to a society's culture. Fine arts and the humanistic disciplines are charged with major responsibilities, but my intention includes a wider range than courses in music and painting and philosophy. In one respect, I am not referring to the academic program primarily or at all but am more concerned with the lifelong impact going to college makes. The look of a college, the presence of green space and old and new buildings, the friends made and the conditions that promote friendships, the values that have tangible outcomes in what we buy and where we live and how we treat ourselves and others — these are what I have in mind in this very broad aim.

Conventionally, professors are only tangentially concerned with these matters. A building is chiefly important as it fits the professor's convenience needs rather than as it may relate to the total physical campus and the academic program. Probably all professors take some pride in or are vexed about campus appearance, though the complaints presidents receive are more about convenience of parking than integrity of architecture. Much of the professor's responsibility is that of the citizen, the same responsibility that supports civic planning and zoning ordinances, that petitions for preservation, that votes and urges others to vote on issues that go beyond services and taxation.

After thirty years of living on and visiting campuses, I can see pluses and minuses in this kind of concern. As compared with the rapid expansion after World War II, colleges are doing better planning, involving the faculty and considering overall design as well as specific desires, and their campuses reflect diverse values beyond the immediate need for enclosed space. However, the internal difficulties of teaching or living on many of the large campuses are patently obvious in the physical plant, as it used to be called. Growth today is seldom plantlike but too often an erection of mechanical parts warring for what little space there is.

The highest aim would be to effect some harmony between the academic program and its physical surroundings. Maybe in years long past, the college on a hill, the rural Athens, attained this harmony. So it might seem with a faculty largely wed to its place, however remote it might be from Göttingen or Cambridge, with students there as residents on their own for the first time, and with both creating a distinctive culture, limited as it may have been. The physical configurations of many such colleges still exist, but those with most claim to academic excellence have been cosmopolitanized despite the setting. That easy ambiance between faculty and students struggles against professional pressures that keep professors and their students at a distance. Still, such institutions do better in these respects than huge universities that have turned small towns into metropolises or have expanded within the limited space and unfavorable conditions that beset huge population centers. Such institutions are marked with an academic urban blight that affects both students and faculty.

As to teaching and the high aims it holds for education, a deliberate emphasis on connectedness, on relationships — on ecology, if you will — seems to be every teacher's responsibility. Holding on to some of the attempts of the sixties to fuse living and learning may be a limited but worthy aim for a college teacher. A larger aim is to resist the persistent notions that classes and study and learning are one thing and having fun and getting stoned and turning up the volume are another. The most important impact a teacher may have, amidst much that for the student is a mere naming of parts, is to bring together for the student those many things that would otherwise remain apart.

By now, most teachers are aware of and respectful toward both the cognitive and affective domains. Recognition of those distinctive traits controlled by the right and left sides of the brain has not so much widened the split in our perceptions as heightened the need for synthesis. College teachers have always had some part in developing the affective side; without colleges and universities the fine arts in this country would be as barren as Mencken claimed they were in the twenties. The arts scarcely existed outside major metropolitan centers then. Today, they flourish in small cities and large throughout the country, though the time has not arrived when an artist can earn a reasonable and steady income in all these places. One might even claim that the universities are over-producing concert performers, dancers, potters, and candlemakers, if the measure is a balance between numbers of artists and craftsmen and adequate levels of support. Nevertheless, the public has been the beneficiary and artists, at the least, have had more opportunities of a kind than ever before.

If this has resulted in a softening of the lines of American culture, it has been in the direction John Adams set forth in 1780: "I must study politics and war that my sons may have liberty to study mathematics and philosophy. My sons ought to study mathematics and philosophy, geography, natural history and naval architecture, navigation, commerce and agriculture, in order to give their children a right to study painting, poetry, music, architecture, statuary, tapestry, and porcelain" (Adams, 1930, p. 67). Such softening may represent a considerable counter to the destructive forces that the cognitive domain continues to build. As the growth of the arts might affect the teacher, I have hopes it might enter into classes seemingly most remote, in which geologists might sing and a chemist act out the drama inherent in the complex combinations of things unseen. The goal is for teachers to recognize their own affective qualities and needs and not to function as mere instruments of measurement and calculation. The growth of the arts in the public sector may have created not only more consumers but also more participants. That vastly important and complex job of civilizing ourselves is visibly continuing on. As higher education, theoretically, catches its students at crucial points of inclination to adult life, it should not set negative examples whereby each teacher's insisting on his or her pound of flesh rules out the possibility of being affected by the larger culture that lies outside professional training.

It is in the arts, too, where questions of valuing, discriminating in a positive sense, can be engagingly and unthreateningly raised. We may heatedly defend our love of Mozart as against Beethoven, but we are not as threatened by our insensitive opponent as if he were building a nuclear waste dump in our backyard. One of the essential issues for a democratic polity is developing citizens able both to discriminate and not to discriminate. Slowly we have moved to confront the social and political discriminations that are inimical to a functioning democratic society. We are only a small way toward being receptive and generous and unjudging and, at the same time, selective and sparing and, yes, discriminating, about most of the manifold aspects that go into the quality of life. The college teacher within a subject matter needs to be expert in both directions, helping students draw together separate perspectives to see an object whole but equally helpful in perceiving and valuing its separate parts. Much of the beauty of an object lies in noticing what the casual observer does not notice, from a surprised attention to its parts. More, it lies in the perceiver's habit, not of looking for points of discrimination as manifestations of superior sight or taste, but rather of responding reflectively and even vagrantly to the particulars of sensory experience and to how these particulars may be ordered. By such inclinations fostered in our students we might, in time, arrive at an artistic culture less directly reflective of the angular, strident, powerful, violent, aggressive, and negative aspects of modern culture.

Teaching Toward Moral Responsibility

Finally, we cannot abandon moral aims for higher education even as we attempt to find ways that skirt the claims of specific religions and ideologies. Teachers, as I have argued throughout, need develop style and character, the one to catch the student's unfocused eye, to use the momentary power of the esthetically pleasing to arrest attention, the other to establish a more lasting connection between one's separate learning and the person one becomes. What one values may be as fully grounded esthetically as cognitively. Though to some degree we may be taught to be good, we are probably good by other measures, including that one so attractive to youth, that if it feels good it must be good. To get the feel of right choice, that is a profound human achievement.

Enough has been said about developing both style and character to make it unnecessary to amplify my meaning as regards the teacher's functioning. The only additional remark is that such individual development is not likely to come without some larger acceptance of morality as fundamental to human development. A former student of Nadia Boulanger, one of the most influential of teachers, notes that her lessons always had "much moral exhortation — as for example, genius without character is nothing; character without genius is nearly everything" (Epstein, 1981, p. 99). College teachers find it too comfortable to apply the supposedly value-free character of their special investigations to the lives they affect. At an extreme, such a teacher draws back, not in humility but in comforting blindness, from claiming to affect the student's larger life. We have a large responsibility only as we have a large claim on the time and strivings of students during a crucially malleable period in their lives. The claim is different from that of their parents. We can exercise no greater responsibility, one fraught with risk and complexity and no sure pattern of proceeding, than that of sanctioning the importance of right choice and conduct. This does not mean creating for students or mandating choices or even "teaching" about right choice. Right choice will not be, for our time, one set of actions under one fixed code, but just as surely it will not be an endorsement of anything goes. That such questions are not a lower order of questions and cannot be taken care of somewhere else may be among the most important learning teachers can accomplish. Individuals cannot abjure the notion of right choosing; the civilization we perilously occupy hangs by a thread on right choice.

As American college teachers are uncomfortable about being charged with moral responsibilities, so are most of them insufficiently sensitive to the part they play in helping develop "fully functioning persons" (Rogers, 1969, pp. 279-297). Thus, in reflecting back upon almost forty years of being subjected to or subjecting others to higher education, I think less about those who — and I am among them — easily adapted to and profited from college going and more about those who did not. I feel in myself the same rising temper that provoked Whitehead to write prior

to 1917: "When one considers in its length and in its breadth the importance of this question of the education of a nation's young, the broken
lives, the defeated hopes, the national failures, which result from the
frivolous inertia with which it is treated, it is difficult to restrain within
oneself a savage rage" (1949, p. 26).

The "frivolous inertia" covers all that customary behavior by
which teachers presume they are performing adequately in only keeping
their specific subject matters before them, in measuring their students'
aptitudes by their own authoritarian definitions of what is to be learned,
and in passing judgment upon their students' whole worth, however they
disguise such judgments as precisely defined measures of individual
accomplishments. Every year of my teaching life has afforded me disturbing specific examples. One such is the fervor with which colleagues
in the sciences and mathematics argued against expunging from the academic record a student's failing grade that was supposedly atoned for by
successfully repeating the course. Nothing less than a public branding—
an F burned into the brow—would do for the most vindictive of these
supposed teachers. Another example is the faculty argument that course
arrangements and calendars have little relation to student learning. Is it
"frivolous inertia" or self-serving that explains the casual attention given
to how courses are packaged, what relationship they bear to a student's
other courses, or how little or long they stretch out? Worst of all is the
failure to share in, contribute to, and keep alive the excitement that the
first exposure to university life can create. What chance of sharing in the
inestimable worth of great beginnings is there in a faculty that has
largely absconded from the vital courses at the moments of potentially
greatest impact? And at the other end of the process—measured, if not
precisely then symptomatically, by the huge numbers of faculty and students who do not bother to attend commencement exercises—is the
sense, largely created by the collective functioning of the faculty, that, by
God, it's over at last. I am haunted, too, by visions of those great numbers still who would like to have had a better chance at college going,
would like not to have had their earlier inadequacies further exposed and
confirmed, would like to have felt encouraged, if not inspired, and, at
the least, not defeated, by prolonging learning into that period where,
with some nurturing, a human plant might flower into some wholeness,
the radiance of the blossom aside.

If I have here and elsewhere been uncharitable to science, it is because of my experiences with broad samplings of faculty in many different colleges and universities for many years and because science sets the prevailing tone for higher education. Perhaps what I am seeing is not confined to the sciences but rather to all those many faculty caught up in the given of formalized education and following it out on the conventional lines of organization and efficiency and tangible results. I have already cited both Jacob Bronowski and René Dubos as men of science wise beyond the specialized subjects in which they are expert. "It may prove difficult," Dubos (1981, p. 228) writes, "to give young people the education that would prepare them for ways of life in which community spirit and some measure of self-sufficiency are as important as is now the acquisition and accumulation of money." Education and learning, he believes, must be both more dispersed throughout society and spread more continuously throughout the life span. He continues: "A humanistic society would prize more highly skills facilitating better human relationships and more creative interplay between humankind, nature and technology. In future societies, the most valuable people might be, not those with the greatest ability to produce material goods, but rather those who have the gift to spread good will and happiness through empathy and understanding. Such a gift may be innate in part but could certainly be enhanced by experience and education" (p. 229).

It is in the sciences that the central problem of dealing with specific intellectual incompetence without destroying human dignity or assailing human worth needs most attention. Somehow, and in the interest of science itself and all that it contributes to human satisfactions, the aims of college teaching must be made both more broad and generous. They must value both highly specialized excellence and a self-development that is not so much discriminating and refined as it is tolerant and accommodating. Reaching such goals, we might arrive at more individuals who experience satisfaction with what they are and do and who are, in Rogers' term, "soundly and realistically social," both necessities for a healthy society.

10

The Sixties and Now

*I*n 1962, I published my first book on education. It was called *The Profane Comedy* and gained a brief period of public notoriety as a biting attack on the establishment. The publisher subtitled it *American Higher Education in the Sixties*, though I had not written it with any such sweeping claim in mind. Rather, the idea for the book grew out of my experiences as student, student and teacher, and teacher over fifteen years at a number of quite different colleges and universities. The driving urge for it came from wanting to get down my views while the student in me was still alive enough to give them thrust and point.

My attention to teaching since then is consistent with that earlier self, though I would be indulging in self-deceit if I did not recognize how much I have been professorized. This book's focus on what I deem the higher mysteries of teaching has entailed some considerations of higher education as it may stand now. Thus, it provides a basis for looking back and making this final chapter a comparison of one student-teacher's views

157

of the way things were then — 1960, to use a round figure — with how they are now, in the 1980s.

Some Comparative Statistics

As the first book began with statistics, so will I begin with comparative figures here. In 1960, about 3,600,000 students, almost one fourth of the college-age population, attended college (the figure was about 4 percent in 1900). Today about 12,000,000 attend, roughly 40 percent of the college-age population. In 1960, about 1,400 colleges and universities granted 400,000 bachelor's or first professional degrees; in 1980, there were about 2,000 such institutions granting 900,000 degrees. In 1960, there were about 600 junior or community colleges giving less than B.A. or B.S. degrees. Today there are over 1,200.

In 1960, the University of California with 54,000 students on seven campuses was the largest institution of this kind; it now has over 130,000 students on nine campuses. Today Ohio State has over 50,000 students on its main campus in Columbus, and at least a dozen universities have enrollments of over 35,000 students on a single campus. The 60 largest campuses, making under 2 percent of the total number, today enroll about 1,875,000 full- and part-time students, about 15 percent of those attending colleges and universities. At the other extreme, colleges with enrollments of fewer than 1,000 are only 39 percent of the total number of institutions now as contrasted with 63 percent in 1960. Enrollments in community and junior colleges were 453,000 in 1960 as against 4,500,000 today, full and part time.

If the system was extensive in 1960, it is even more vast and diverse now, with extremes far apart. Higher education has expanded outward and upward, fueled principally by the great college-age population bulge that began in the 1960s. Though retrenchment has been a major concern of the eighties, its particular effects do little to modify the overall picture of great growth in the past twenty years. With all institutions pressed financially, signs are arising that some institutions will begin to limit enrollments. Ohio State's board of regents, for example, in 1982, imposed a limit of 40,000 full-time equivalent undergraduates on the Columbus campus. Colorado's state legislature that same year imposed a limit of 13,500 in-state full-time equivalent students at the University of Colorado, with a fine to be imposed for exceeding that figure.

Elsewhere at large public universities, where branch campuses have not already spread out great numbers, raising admissions requirements has been another way of both limiting and selecting students.

Statistics that compare 1960 to today give support to generalizations that have significance for college teachers and students:

- Public colleges and universities continue to enroll the greatest percentage of students, and the large public universities the greatest percentage of those.
- Community colleges have greatly increased in number and in number of students enrolled, largely a result of public policy in the separate states beginning in the sixties.
- Single college campuses have gone beyond the numbers of students that can be accommodated in any easy way; the adverse effects on undergraduate education have not yet received the attention they deserve.
- Private colleges, large and small, have probably lost the influence they once had and play a comparatively smaller role in education at both the beginning and the graduate levels.
- An increasing percentage of schools have become part of the universities offering doctoral programs, despite the shortage of academic positions in many fields. The four-year liberal arts college has lost most in comparison to the growth of institutions on either side.

Limbo, Purgatory, and Paradise

One other general observation can be related to these statistics and to the metaphor—the profane comedy—used in my first book. In 1962, classifying colleges into Limbo, Purgatory, and Paradise seemed to represent the attitudes of many young professors like myself toward the profession they were about to enter. There was no Inferno, for American colleges were too optimistically bent on secular salvation to grant the existence of Hell. Limbo, I wrote, constituted the "lowest level of American colleges where the educational vagrants, the intellectual pagans, the good but academically unsanctified are assigned." It included primarily the small colleges with normal school or denominational ties in their backgrounds. To young professors out of graduate school, these colleges seemed to be at the edge of the academic cosmos; a permanent existence there was an assignment to oblivion. Such colleges still exist in great numbers today. My hopes for mergers and consolidations were in vain; in many states, a tier of public community colleges was erected on top of a surfeit of struggling four-year colleges. The distance between these colleges and the graduate schools is still great. The struggle for funds is intense and, of late, the struggle to get students as well, and the faculties are still beset with feelings of isolation from and inferiority to those larger public colleges and universities that most students attend.

Despite this basic sameness and the aptness of earlier criticisms — their expediency, provinciality, administrative autocracy, low standards for both students and faculty — I feel more can be said for these colleges now than I said then. The flush times for graduate work in the sixties has clearly improved faculties in these institutions, even though at present there is much concern about the future effects of tenuring. The disaffection of some faculty members, whose graduate work and accomplishments created higher expectations, may be greater, particularly as they have less chance of moving elsewhere. Still, my limited observations point in another direction: the energies of very good faculty members going into making the most of institutions limited in almost every other way — physical facilities, library holdings, cultural milieu, financing. Moreover, the kind of teaching I have been championing seems to have a chance to go on and is going on in many of these colleges. Quite independent of my own observations, Martin (1982, p. 21) has recently concluded that "the revival of intermediate and mediating institutions in American life" depends on the vigorous survival of these same small liberal arts colleges.

Professors at such institutions always did and still do teach a great deal. Necessity in the recent past led many to adopt courses, programs, calendars, grading practices, and the like at variance with traditional practices and more attuned to the diverse ways of students' learning. The environment supports a faculty member's commitment to teaching, unless, of course, the drive to imitate institutions of more eminence is strong. The narrowness of community morality, in itself affected by changes of the sixties, rests less heavily on the faculty, and so, to a degree, does the authoritarian hand of administration. Finally, from the students' point of view, these colleges, were it not that so many are private and therefore compelled to charge relatively high tuitions, offer attractive alternatives to the huge public institutions that still enroll the largest single group of students. The reality that high tuitions limit student choice comes through in a survey (*Chronicle of Higher Education*, 1982, p. 1) of 122 private colleges and universities with enrollments over 500 which showed a drop of 39 percent from 1979 to 1981 in enrollments of students from families with annual income between $6,000 and $24,000. Average student expense — tuition, board and room — rose from $5,800 to $7,211 during that period.

When I surveyed Purgatory in 1960, I included all that great number of colleges and universities somewhere between Limbo and "the handful of first-rate universities of which this country can boast." Professors in these institutions, mostly public supported and vocationally oriented, "feel a sense of strain at being pumpers of intellectual gas, caught up in genteel poverty, dogged by departmental feuds, faced with challenges neither they nor the institutions they serve are quite up to." Most of these institutions have become larger; many have upgraded themselves by conventional academic measures — offering M.A. and even Ph.D. degree programs — and like the colleges of Limbo, have probably improved faculty by measures of highest degree held and evidence of specialized competence. My acquaintance with many of these universities today finds them not much better or worse by my measures than they were then. I am more sympathetic with their emphasis upon work and study, their ties with social aims and values, and their representing in teaching some of the broad aims discussed in the previous chapter. At worst, many of them have relapsed into State U. as seen in thirties movies, a respectable place for the local population's gentry to attend if they cannot opt for attendance at more prestigious universities elsewhere. At such institutions, the academic programs and faculty behavior still ape those of the great and famous universities, even though both entail debilitating conflicts with an unselected student body, an administrative bureaucracy, and a curriculum that defies rational explanation.

My own values reverse common academic ones. In recent visits to many of these campuses, I find more to praise in those institutions most in harmony with the actualities of the public that surrounds and supports them than in those that have pitched their aims at national prestige. The reasons for such flouting of customary ratings of institutions are many. My emphasis is upon teaching, and institutions bent on achieving national prestige are often both hostile toward and arrogant about undergraduate teaching. Moreover, a learning community is not a hollow ideal. A gypsy faculty, or one that would be such were circumstances favorable, does not create community or foster learning that has some wholeness and center for the students it serves.

As to Paradise, my conception in 1960 was a rarefied one: "The dozen or so schools which attract faculties with international reputations, pay them well, and enable them to contribute to the intellectual life of the country out of all proportion to their numbers." I am not so impressed with these universities as I once was. Many of them are basically inhospitable to teaching and set patterns badly imitated by lesser institutions and seriously flawed in themselves. Whether we look at the youth culture of the sixties or the industrial-technological culture those youths railed against, both are more creations of universities singled out for their highest excellence than of institutions of any other kind. Paradise, by this measure, seems a strange identification indeed. I may have been seduced to some degree by the high percentage of students — 90 percent in 1960 — graduating from such institutions and by a corollary that was probably not true then and is certainly not true now, that every graduate "can write reasonably well, think with some precision and some tenacity, and read and have an idea of what is worth reading."

Paradise, chiefly in terms of research facilities and accomplishments, has probably expanded since the 1960s. The latest evaluation of doctoral programs (*An Assessment of Research Doctorate Programs...* , 1983) expands the number of universities that have doctoral programs in at least some subject matter areas that compare favorably with those at the highest-ranked institutions. The lack of surprise in the universities that rank at the top makes one wonder what besides vanity justifies the making of such surveys. The top ten graduate schools according to these composite ratings are the same now as in 1970, with the University of California at Berkeley, Stanford, Harvard, Yale, and the Massachusetts Institute of Technology the top five. Some further support for believing there has been an expansion at the top comes from looking at salaries. In 1960–61, only four universities were paying an average compensation of $11,000 and above. Setting a comparable figure at $30,700, the average compensation in 1980 of all faculty in the top category of institutions participating in the AAUP salary survey (American Association of University Professors, 1981), 213 institutions were included in this category. At the other end of financing, increases in tuition and fees at the private colleges among these have placed them even more out of the reach of all but the moneyed classes. The specialness of these schools in this respect has become more special still, and this despite the attempts of many of them to maintain scholarship programs, to encourage minorities, and to draw from a national pool. As to the broad aims of education as I have conceived them, these schools have not in the past shown the leadership that might be expected, nor do they promise to do so in the future. They are most tied to the theology of knowledge, which I think needs drastic reform.

The Professoriate Then and Now

In 1960, college teaching was something of a peculiar profession, perhaps because of the oddity of thinking as a way to earn a living. It is less odd now. The "knowledge industry" has expanded greatly in two decades. Going to college has become even more the normal course for college-age youth. Occupations have been increasingly professionalized. And professors have simply become more numerous, an estimated 690,000 full- and part-time college teachers at instructor level and above in 1981, as against 236,000 in 1960. As a consequence of this, the profession has gained wider public acceptance and professors feel less strange about their occupation. Nevertheless, a national study (Magarrell, 1982) reports a decline in faculty morale during the seventies seemingly unrelated to salaries but connected with dissatisfactions about playing meaningful roles in the governance and direction of their institutions.

The biggest change since 1960 is clearly in the prospects awaiting new professors then and now. Though the fifties had a period in which jobs in many disciplines were hard to find, the market in the sixties was overwhelmingly favorable to faculty — with one qualification, however. Even in the days when professors were in demand, positions of the most desirable kind were not very abundant. Most Ph.D.s took the route of moving from an institution of great prestige and high intellectual caliber and often within a heady cultural milieu to much less invigorating climates and to positions that involved much teaching at a basic level. That adjustment is probably even harder to make today, tempered, if at all, by thoughts of large numbers of colleagues unable to get any kind of academic job. That other kind of limbo, the floating faculty who move from one temporary position to another, or who take other jobs but keep their hand in by accepting part-time employment, scarcely existed in the sixties. These changes in prospects have made the profession much less attractive to those most directly affected by these conditions and who might have been expected to set more store by teaching. At the same time, reduced mobility has strengthened pressure on young faculty to publish, to become visible by this route in order to find a better place.

On the whole, the professoriate looks no better in terms of salaries to those entering it today than it did in 1960. Instructors were receiving around $5,700 in salary and fringe benefits in 1960, as compared with $5,620 median income for families in the United States. In 1980, instructor compensation was about $17,700, as compared with a national median family income of about $20,000 (American Association of University Professors, 1980; U.S. Bureau of the Census, 1982). Other figures in our time may affect faculty perspectives adversely: comparisons with salaries of nonacademic professionals (Krishne and Marsh, 1981; American Association of University Professors, 1982) and the huge salaries going to professional athletes, for example. Academics in the sixties could still joke about athletes who could do everything with a basketball but autograph it. It is hard to joke about athletes now who may be only as skilled and as smart as it takes to get rich.

Student Life and Attitudes

The resurgence of sororities and fraternities, the flocking to schools of business and to computer technology, the preoccupation with grades that will supposedly open doors to the professions, the diminished concern for social and political action are all marks of a great shift in student attitudes from the late sixties to today. Already in 1960, observers noted a decline in interest in student groups, clubs, and fraternities; by 1968, all except politically activist groups were passé on many campuses. If there is any norm for American college students, the student of the eighties and the early sixties may be close to it. Today, "activities" are reappearing in force, and not much different in kind from those that celebrated college life in the thirties.

Though organized student life has returned, the sheer size of so many universities is not likely to favor any large percentage of participation. At the University of Utah, where student government has traditionally been strong, less than 6 percent of students participated in the last election. Only 450 out of some 23,000 students filled out a request for student opinion about appropriate speakers for a student-supported lecture series. Carl Sagan, Richard Nixon, Lee Iacocca, and David Letterman led the list. Students' experiences in such institutions may be not unlike that for faculty: a sense of not knowing anyone except those in one's immediate classes or formal social group, and the size and scope of that group's activities dwindling into insignificance against the mass. Many faculty have made a virtue of this isolation by retreating into a privatism that gets the work done that will secure them tenure or advancement but disengages them from the larger issues of education. Students may be more susceptible to efforts made to give them an identity within the mass. The time is very favorable for faculty to function more fully as teachers, helping to increase the students' commitment to their academic work by playing on the need for identity, increasing opportunities for faculty and students to work together in academic contexts of formal and informal kinds.

At the same time, teachers right now probably have to provide more motivation for students, particularly in interesting them in studies outside their career goals. Greater engagement of students in outside activities and in working to pay for college costs will also make the teacher's task harder. David Riesman's *On Higher Education* (1981) is chiefly concerned with the complex and shifting relationships between students and the colleges they attend. He describes current students as "passive in the sense that they will not be intellectually engaged with what they are studying" (p. 313), but notes that such intellectual engagement has never been common among students in the United States. Their aims, he goes on, "have always been, like those of most of their teachers, either directly or covertly pragmatic and utilitarian." If students are serious today, they are serious in conventional ways. Grades and test scores loom large but hardly measure, if they ever did, a commitment to an engaged and large-minded learning. Professors who lived through the sixties lamented the apathy that seemed to be the most marked characteristic of students by the mid seventies. Having resisted the excesses of passion that got in the way of academic work in the sixties, the same professor now found himself having to stir them up. It is ever so. No teacher has for long found student motivation wholly self-creating. Motivating and stimulating students will be a necessity for the effective teacher of the eighties.

Athletics

I have touched briefly on college athletics in talking about academic hypocrisies. In the early sixties, recruiting was just gaining attention as a major source of winning teams and unethical practices. Currently (1983), college presidents, who even more than the collective faculty have let college athletics become what they are, play a large part in two major panels investigating intercollegiate sports. "The basic issue is how to maintain the integrity of universities," the executive director of the National Collegiate Athletic Association (NCAA) committee said (Vance, 1982b, p. 1). That note has been sounded in all the major investigations, their history stretching back almost as far as the history of intercollegiate athletics itself. From the perspective of today, my 1960 examination of the adverse consequences of recruiting and the increasing distance between big-time athletes and students fell short of anticipating current practices. Certainly the NCAA is stronger, but it is questionable that either its policies or structure can preserve academic integrity. Moreover, it is even doubtful that it can control the infractions against its own permissive policies.

I am not referring to the kind of breaking of rules that caused the president of the University of San Francisco, the Rev. John Lo Schiavo, to explain the ending of intercollegiate basketball after fifty-eight years because USF "cannot afford to pay the price the basketball program is imposing on it. That price is being exacted in terms much more important than money" (*Chronicle of Higher Education*, August 11, 1982, p. 12). I am speaking of the array of practices legalized by the NCAA — financial aid, recruiting, redshirting, progress toward degrees, tutoring, scheduling, domiciling, and feeding — that mark the NCAA's regulating of athletics since the Carnegie investigation of 1929.

The problem is a vexing one, an indication of how little control the university may have over certain driving forces, whether they be athletes gone public and professional, or scholarship in league with both trivial and destructive ends. In either instance, the responsibility is not the university's alone. And yet as regards athletics, faculty, administrators, students, and alumni must share the blame with athletic directors, coaches, equipment manufacturers, promoters, and gamblers, to name only those closest to the exhilaration of athletic competition and the corruption that seems to follow.

Current criticism of the numbers of athletes who fail to get degrees has elicited statistics arousing some hope that institutions can still keep athletics related to academic work. Graduation rates of senior regulars on top basketball teams, according to *The Sporting News*, varied from 100 percent in the Ivy League to 30 percent in the Big Ten (*Chronicle of Higher Education*, November 3, 1982). The commissioner of the Big East Conference, where 77 percent were graduated, observed, "The biggest single difference over the years is that the athletic departments in the East operate with a lesser degree of independence in the structure of the university" (p. 17).

Periodically, individual institutions and national bodies will tighten the academic regulations governing admission of athletes and their progress to a degree. Faculty in the sixties were about as easily bypassed in these matters as they are today. In both periods, offenders were occasionally caught, their numbers including faculty and administrators, coaches and staff, and athletes themselves. Over two decades, requirements for athletic eligibility have been raised slightly, eliciting justified controversy at present about the discriminatory effects upon black athletes.

But the hottest topic for all those heavily engaged in big-time sports today is what to do with all that money coming in from television. "If money is the root of all evil," says Stanley Ward (in Vance, 1982a, p. 16), general counsel for the University of Oklahoma, "it's also the mother's milk of college athletics." He speaks the truth. Ties with television and through that to professional sports and through that to big money and enterprise have fastened this corruption on colleges and universities with little chance of reform or redemption.

Remedial Work

In 1960, remedial courses — crudely called "bonehead" courses — were requiring the energies of a great many faculty. Most faculty avoided them if they could, grudgingly took them on when they could not. As the sixties went on, the remedial problem seemed to disappear, maybe because standards of all kinds were relaxed or, more likely, because rapid growth made it possible for the majority of the faculty to escape altogether from this level of work while a rising number of graduate assistants created just the stoop labor to handle it. But the problem did not really go away. Looking back, I think most of what I wrote about this subject in 1960 was wrong, except for proposing a new kind of college whose program would acknowledge both the deficiencies many students bring with them and the useful ends for which they might prepare. Even that proposal was much too simple and too condescending, although in some ways the development of community colleges has been in the direction I had in mind.

In the present confrontation with remedial work, many colleges and universities act as if it were a new phenomenon, despite the fact that intelligent and devoted work has been going on in some universities all the while. Moreover, "bonehead" seems to have been extended to much of the college population. Not much is new, nor was it in 1960, except as to numbers. College students have never come to college as well prepared as faculty would like. American education's continuing expansion has always brought new groups into higher levels of schooling who do not fit requirements fashioned for a more select group; writing has always been a hard skill to acquire, and mathematics is still tough. In 1960, I could think it possible to push remedial education aside or to get tough with the unprepared or deficient student. "No higher educational institution should exist without some standard of admission," I wrote high-mindedly then. Events have proved me wrong. We have opened doors and will probably keep them open, though students will still find many of them closed. Most dramatically but still not fully, we have opened doors to those barred by race, though in retrospect it seems incredible that it should have taken that long.

If I am uneasy about "standards" today, it is because over the years I have seen them too much linked with barriers of race and money and sex and social position. I should have recognized then the linkage between required remedial work and the limiting of access for those many students who did not meet traditional academic standards. Though remedial students could be regarded as composing a cross section of the college population, that cross section was heavily weighted with minority groups already the victims of discrimination in other ways.

Within my own field, we have learned much about the complex of causes that lies behind reading and writing deficiencies and something about how to help students overcome these problems. We have also learned that professors are no more inclined to embrace remedial work now than they were in the sixties. If anything has changed, it is that dissatisfactions with the verbal abilities students demonstrate at entrance (and even at graduation) are spread over a wider range of faculty. To a degree, it is also recognized that students who cannot read and write well or who do not function well in other classrooms may not be simply dumbbells or boneheads. The questions remain unanswered as to how best to treat failing students in any subject. My own stance as a teacher has been steadily to try to diminish the numbers of failures, to recognize and intervene before failure is confirmed, to search out what special kind of help might be useful, and, when nothing else avails, at least to arrive at some understanding of what underlies the student's poor performance rather than simply to cross her off, flunk him out. Perhaps this is a sign of soft-headedness associated with growing old. Or perhaps I am growing up to embrace larger responsibilities as both a human being and a teacher.

Unresolved Problems

Another topic that gives me as much distress now as it did then is the faculty's ability to live with problems perpetually posed but never solved. Remedial instruction is one such problem, but so are grades and the assigning of credit; the curriculum is always a problem and a worse one now than in 1960; the reward system is a chronic problem and creator of problems; the conduct of athletics is more than a problem. Some basic reasons I arrived at then probably hold with more force today: the temper of the academic mind, the balancing of powers within the university, the bureaucracy that keeps everything in place, the dominance of committees and the absence of leadership, the shape of the calendar, the divided attention of the faculty.

The only forces for consequential change that I have observed during my career resulted from the influx of veterans after World War II and from the explosion of students in the sixties. No such forces exist for consequential changes in this decade. It would be enough for me to look back at the end of the eighties and find that college professors had preserved some of the earlier changes that seem most beneficial to teaching and learning. It will not be easy to turn college students back into children, for what the veterans forced upon faculty — that they were grown up and intelligent and must be dealt with as such — was reinforced by students of the sixties, even though many were not grown up and not very intelligent. Nevertheless, teaching has become more a matter of faculty-student interchange rather than authoritarian instuction. My long-maintained call for the end of grading and credit hours was made more from indignation than from expectation of change. Yet, the sixties did break the stranglehold of grades to some degree and even broke courses loose from rigid patterns. Both are threatened today by a faculty's fondness for reverting back to some purer state. If teachers can but preserve the pass-fail option for some courses and for a variety of learning purposes, that will be a great gain. If they could go further and see that, though this concession was dragged out of the faculty by the students, it is very much the faculty's business to consider where grades are appropriate and useful and necessary and where they are not, that would be progress. As to courses, many of the small colleges have stuck to interim terms of various kinds and have used them intelligently and imaginatively to foster new approaches to subject matter, varied types of experiential learning, different modes of learning, and combinations of travel and study vital to breaking down both faculty and student provincialism. Even that small space in which to vary favorably teaching and learning is worth fighting to preserve. It seems fairly clear by now that the small number of experimental colleges that came into existence in the sixties will not increase in the eighties (Cowley, 1981). Some of the existing ones may not survive or may revert to practices much closer to the mass of institutions. One is left with a paradox: though teaching by its very nature is designed to bring about change in the student, professors in the main strongly resist change in themselves and in the routines that define their teaching.

Achievements

Finally, I think the achievements I singled out for American colleges and universities in the sixties are no less remarkable today. Higher education has been extended to a larger portion of society than in any other civilization, past or present. It has provided centers for cultural enrichment as well as for professional and vocational training necessary to a technological society. It has in the large kept faith with the democratic ideals of equal opportunity for all. It has moved America away from provincialism, and despite being one of the principal engines of a consuming society, it has helped maintain a persistent and tough American idealism.

What the professoriate has achieved as teachers is less easy to single out. No startling changes in pedagogy, either through experience or research, have come about in twenty years. In the longer span of American colleges and universities, teaching has become more of an interactive rather than inculcative practice. As has been noted, this change may have come about in part because of the influx of veterans after World War II. The acceptance of student evaluation by a majority of collegiate institutions is a tangible sign of such a shift, for no such wide acceptance can be found in previous periods.

In denying startling changes in pedagogy, I am not blind to the considerable range of technological innovations, most of which have developed in the past thirty years. Television has become more sophisticated and adaptable to more educational purposes. The computer appears to have a similar growth and promise. The possibilities of both, and of other obviously useful aids to learning, continue to create some stir about the completely automated college and university, one of the commoner fantasies of educational futurists. The failure of the University of Mid-America (Watkins, 1982), established in 1974 to develop a media course network that might expand into an American Open University, is significant in this respect. Despite a consortium of eleven universities, government funding, a firm precedent in England's Open University, American technology, and an American population dispersed over considerable distances, its efforts did not succeed. Obviously, human beings can learn vastly more than they do learn and can learn it without the time and trouble of going to college. Were colleges and universities not both socially and culturally attractive, television and computers would already play a much larger role in education than they do. But such technology has only, however spectacularly, expanded opportunities that have been within human capacities for a long time. The crucial questions are: Will people learn on their own? How to get them to learn? What do they want to learn? What should they want to learn? The socialization that attends college going is something technology cannot provide, and the very presence of technology may make that socialization ever more desirable. Technological innovations expand the capacity of a teacher to do some of the specific jobs at hand, but they work best when the capacities of the teacher fully embrace the complexities and satisfactions of teaching and learning as a human exchange.

The full impact of the "information revolution" on colleges and universities is likely to be larger and more varied than specific changes in pedagogy. Libraries and scholarly research are already greatly affected by vastly improved capacities for storing and retrieving information. Student learning is being radically changed by the cheap availability of pocket calculators. The capacities for society at large, outside the walls of formal educational institutions, to gain useful information and useful skills expand day by day. But, just to focus on these obvious changes, advances in technology are not necessarily advances in higher learning. Libraries have never been fully integrated into the teaching program despite their long existence at the center of the college campus. There is already a mass of research of dubious worth generated and disseminated by the printed word. The overwhelming presence of calculators of all kinds surely has much to do with student resistance to mathematics. And as yet, an ability to identify numbers and press buttons does not seem to be a necessary grounding in mathematics upon which much advanced technology depends. Finally, the increasing capacity of all societies to process and disseminate information increases perils associated with its use and the necessity for developing not only national but global citizenship.

The themes I have emphasized in this book about teaching seem somewhat more important to me now than they were in the sixties, but they are important at any time. One is the need to recognize the essentially personal in teaching, neither to trivialize it nor let it be submerged under mere technical training or objective scholarship. Another is to recognize that teaching carries with it the obligation that any teacher is developing more than a subject matter competence, is an agent in developing, for want of a better word, *character* in the student, and therefore must look to developing his or her own character in becoming a teacher of stature. If teachers believe, as I do, in the promise of democracy, then they must acknowledge the unavoidable connection between teaching and the developing of citizens and a democratic society. Another theme emphasized in this book is the need to make more of the joys and pleasures of teaching, to fight the dead hand of institutionalizing and our own tendencies to make learning hurt. Another is to let our teaching be more informed by keeping ourselves alive as learners, by forcing upon ourselves the difficulties and satisfactions of being students. A large cluster of themes embraces the divided character of much that teachers do: the need to harmonize scholarship and teaching if we can, to give teaching its due if we cannot, and to create a climate in which teaching of many things at many levels to many ends is recognized for the values each has and not as they may be measured by any single received standard.

Throughout the writing of this book, I was drawn to the idea of calling it "Teaching for Survival" and of bending its content to that central purpose. Survival in this instance does not refer to survival of the teacher in a hostile milieu, as might be written of public school teaching, but survival of our species. The specific charge of examining the very place and pursuit of knowledge has no less at stake. I devoutly hope such an examination will begin to take place in force, will begin to affect the particulars of teaching as any major shift in philosophy should have an effect. Community, humane learning, citizenship, a commitment to learning in its actual effects rather than in its shaping of the teacher's career—these are central. If I have kept away from making this altogether a polemic, it is probably because of some residual optimism that has kept many teachers at apparently impossible tasks. For we cannot be sure of perishing and thus we must value teaching for the joys of simply learning as well as for what present and future profits it may yield. In this context, the sins I cite are marks of human imperfection which the optimist in me says may be reduced, if not remedied. The humbler intention for which this book settles is not that it will save some teacher's immortal soul but that it might help save some student worldly pain.

Bibliography

Adams, J. T. *The Adams Family.* New York: Blue Ribbon Books, 1930.

Allen, D. C. *The Ph.D. in English and American Literature.* New York: Holt, Rinehart and Winston, 1968.

American Association of University Professors. *Annual Report of the Economic Status of the Profession.* Washington, D.C.: American Association of University Professors, 1960–1982.

American Council on Education. *Fact Book for Academic Administrators, 1981–1982.* Washington, D.C.: American Council on Education, 1981.

An Assessment of Research Doctorate Programs in the United States. Washington, D.C.: National Academy Press, 1983.

Anderson, J. "The Teacher as Model." *American Scholar,* 1961, *30,* 393–398, 400–401.

Astin, A. W. *Four Critical Years: Effects of College on Beliefs, Attitudes, and Knowledge.* San Francisco: Jossey-Bass, 1977.

Axelrod, J. *The University Teacher As Artist: Toward an Aesthetics of Teaching with Emphasis on the Humanities.* San Francisco: Jossey-Bass, 1973.

Axelrod, J. "From Counterculture to Counterrevolution: A Teaching Career." In K. E. Eble (Ed.), *New Directions for Teaching and Learning: Improving Teaching Styles,* no. 1. San Franscisco: Jossey-Bass, 1980.

Bacon, F. *The Advancement of Learning.* In J. Spedding, R. L. Ellis, and D. D. Heath (Eds.), *The Works of Francis Bacon.* Vol. 3: *Philosophical Works.* New York: Garrett Press, 1968. (Originally published London, 1857-1874.)

Baldwin, R. G., and Blackburn, R. T. "The Academic Career As a Development Process: Implications for Higher Education." *Journal of Higher Education,* 1981, *52* (6), 598-614.

Bate, W. J. "The Crisis in English Studies." *Harvard Magazine,* Sept.- Oct. 1982, pp. 46-53.

Blackburn, R. T. "Career Phases and Their Influence on Faculty Motivation." In J. L. Bess (Ed.), *New Directions for Teaching and Learning: Motivating Professors to Teach Effectively,* no. 10. San Francisco: Jossey-Bass, 1982.

Boyer, E. L., and Hechinger, F. *Higher Learning in the National Interest.* Washington, D. C.: Carnegie Foundation for the Advancement of Teaching, 1981.

Brockway, G. P. "John William Miller." *American Scholar,* Spring 1980, *49,* 236-240.

Bronowski, J. *The Ascent of Man.* Boston: Little, Brown, 1973.

Buscaglia, L. *Living, Loving & Learning.* Thorofare, N.J.: Slack, 1982.

Callahan, D., and Bok, S. (Eds.). *Ethics Teaching in Higher Education.* New York: Plenum, 1980.

Ceci, S. J., and Peters, D. P. "Peer Review: A Study of Reliability." *Change,* 1982, *14* (6), 44-48.

Centra, J. A. *Faculty Development Practices in U.S. Colleges and Universities.* Princeton, N.J.: Educational Testing Service, 1976.

Centra, J. A. *Determining Faculty Effectiveness: Assessing Teaching, Research, and Service for Personnel Decisions and Improvement.* San Francisco: Jossey-Bass, 1979.

Charbonnier, G. (Ed.). *Conversations with Claude Lévi-Strauss.* (J. Weightman and D. Weightman, Trans.) London: Jonathan Cape, 1969.

Chickering, A. W. *Education and Identity.* San Francisco: Jossey-Bass, 1969.

Cole, J. R., and Cole, S. "The Ortega Hypothesis: Citation Analysis Suggests That Only a Few Scientists Contribute to Scientific Progress." *Science,* 1972, *178* (4059), 368-375.

Collins, M. J. (Ed.). *New Directions for Teaching and Learning: Confronting Values and Ethics in College,* no. 13. San Francisco: Jossey-Bass, 1983.

Costin, F., Greenough, W. T., and Menges, R. J. "Student Ratings of College Teaching: Reliability, Validity, and Usefulness." *Review of Educational Research,* 1971, *41,* 511–536.

Cowley, G. "Few 'Alternative' Colleges of the 60s Still Experiment." *Chronicle of Higher Education,* Sept. 23, 1981, pp. 1, 10.

Csikszentmihalyi, M. *Beyond Boredom and Anxiety: The Experience of Play in Work and Games.* San Francisco: Jossey-Bass, 1975.

Csikszentmihalyi, M. "Intrinsic Motivation and Effective Teaching: A Flow Analysis." In J. L. Bess (Ed.), *New Directions for Teaching and Learning: Motivating Professors to Teach Effectively,* no. 10. San Francisco: Jossey-Bass, 1982.

Dolar, M. "Sex Professor at Long Beach Resigns Post." *Los Angeles Times,* June 4, 1982, Part II, Metro.

Dressel, P. L., and Marcus, D. *On Teaching and Learning in College: Reemphasizing the Roles of Learners and the Disciplines in Liberal Education.* San Francisco: Jossey-Bass, 1982.

Dubos, R. *Celebrations of Life.* New York: McGraw-Hill, 1981.

Eble, K. E. *The Profane Comedy: American Higher Education in the Sixties.* New York: Macmillan, 1962.

Eble, K. E. *The Craft of Teaching: A Guide to Mastering the Professor's Art.* San Francisco: Jossey-Bass, 1976.

Epstein, J. (Ed.). *Masters: Portraits of Great Teachers.* New York: Basic Books, 1981.

Erickson, B. L., and Erickson, G. R. "Working with Faculty Teaching Behaviors." In K. E. Eble (Ed.), *New Directions for Teaching and Learning: Improving Teaching Styles,* no. 1. San Francisco: Jossey-Bass, 1980.

Faunce, W. H. P. In *Fiftieth Anniversary of the Opening of Vassar College, October 10 to 13, 1915.* Poughkeepsie, N.Y.: Vassar College, 1916.

"Fighting Lechery on Campus." *Time,* Feb. 4, 1980, p. 84.

Fink, L. D. *First Year on the Faculty: A Study of 100 Beginning College Teachers.* ERIC ED 222 109. 1982.

Foucalt, M. *Power/Knowledge: Selected Interviews and Other Writings, 1972–1977.* (C. Gordon, Trans.) Brighton, England: Harvester Press, 1980.

French-Lazovik, G. (Ed.). *New Directions for Teaching and Learning: Practices that Improve Teaching Evaluation,* no. 11. San Francisco: Jossey-Bass, 1982.

Friedrich, R. J., and Michalak, S. J., Jr. "Why Doesn't Research Improve Teaching?" *Journal of Higher Education,* 1983, *54* (2), 145–162.

Granrose, J. T. "Conscious Teaching: Helping Graduate Assistants Develop Teaching Styles." In K. E. Eble (Ed.), *New Directions for Teaching and Learning: Improving Teaching Styles,* no. 1. San Francisco: Jossey-Bass, 1980.

Grant, W. V., and Eiden, L. J. *Digest of Education Statistics 1982.* Washington, D.C.: National Center for Education Statistics, 1982.

Gullette, M. M. (Ed.). *The Art and Craft of Teaching.* Cambridge, Mass.: Harvard-Danforth Center for Teaching and Learning, 1982.

Hall, R. M., and Sandler, B. R. "The Classroom Climate: A Chilly One for Women?" Project on the Status and Education of Women. Washington, D.C.: Association of American Colleges, 1982.

Hardison, O. B., Jr. *Entering the Maze: Identity and Change in Modern Culture.* New York: Oxford University Press, 1981.

The Hastings Center. *The Teaching of Ethics in Higher Education.* Hastings-on-Hudson, N.Y.: Institute of Society, Ethics, and the Life Sciences, 1980.

Hawkins, H. "University Identity: The Teaching and Research Functions." In A. Oleson and J. Voss (Eds.), *The Organization of Knowledge in Modern America, 1860–1920.* Baltimore: Johns Hopkins University Press, 1979.

Heilbrun, C. G. "Men Over Forty, Women Under Forty." *Chronicle of Higher Education,* Nov. 15, 1976, p. 32.

Highet, G. *The Art of Teaching.* New York: Knopf, 1950.

Hildebrand, M., and others. *Evaluating University Teaching.* Berkeley: Center for Research and Development in Higher Education, University of California, 1971.

Hill, N. K. "Scaling the Heights: The Teacher as Mountaineer." *Chronicle of Higher Education,* June 16, 1980, p. 48.

Hofstadter, R. *Anti-intellectualism in American Life.* New York: Knopf, 1963.

Homer. *Odyssey.* In *Complete Works of Homer.* (S. H. Butcher and A. Lang, Trans.) New York: Modern Library, 1933.

Ionesco, E. *Four Plays by Eugène Ionesco: The Bald Soprano, The Lesson, Jack, or the Submission, The Chairs.* (D. M. Allen, Trans.) New York: Grove Press, 1958.

Jaeger, W. *Paideia: The Ideals of Greek Culture.* (G. Highet, Trans.) Oxford, England: Basil Blackwell, 1946.

Jaques-Dalcroze, E. *Rhythm, Music, and Education.* (H. F. Rubinstein, Trans.) New York: Putnam's, 1921.

Jencks, C., and Riesman, D. *The Academic Revolution.* New York: Doubleday, 1968.

Katz, C. "'Half the Smart People in the Country...'" *Columbia — Magazine of Columbia University,* Oct. 1982, pp. 20–23.

Krishne, E. D., and Marsh, H. W. "Faculty Earnings Compared with Those of Nonacademic Professionals." *Journal of Higher Education,* 1981, *52* (6), 615–623.

Kulik, J. A., and McKeachie, W. J. "The Evaluation of Teachers in Higher Education." In F. N. Kerlinger (Ed.), *Review of Research in Education.* Vol. 3. Itaska, Ill.: Peacock, 1967.

Long, F. A. "Interdisciplinary Problem-Oriented Research in the University." *Science,* 1971, *171,* 961.

Lucas, F. L. *Style.* New York: Collier, 1962.

McKeachie, W. J. *Teaching Tips: A Guidebook for the Beginning College Teacher.* (6th ed.) Lexington, Mass.: Heath, 1969.

McKeachie, W. J. "Student Ratings of Faculty: A Reprise." *Academe,* 1979, *65,* 384–397.

Magarrell, J. "Decline in Faculty Morale Laid to Governance Role, Not Salary." *Chronicle of Higher Education,* Nov. 10, 1982, pp. 1, 28.

Martin, W. B. *A College of Character.* San Francisco: Jossey-Bass, 1982.

Michalak, S. J., and Friedrich, R. J., Jr. "Research Productivity and Teaching Effectiveness at a Small Liberal Arts College." *Journal of Higher Education,* 1981, *52* (6), 578–597.

Millman, J. (Ed.). *Handbook of Teacher Evaluation.* Beverly Hills, Calif.: Sage, 1981.

Myers, I. B. *Introduction to Type.* Palo Alto, Calif.: Consulting Psychologists Press, 1980.

National Board on Graduate Education. *Outlooks and Opportunities for Graduate Education.* Washington, D.C.: National Academy of Sciences, 1976.

"Newman Unit's Report on Graduate Education." *Chronicle of Higher Education,* Mar. 12, 1973, pp. 17–27.

Oakeshott, M. J. *Rationalism in Politics, and Other Essays.* New York: Basic Books, 1962.

Overall, J. U., IV, and Marsh, H. W. "Students' Evaluations of Teaching: An Update." AAHE-ERIC Higher Education Research Currents, *AAHE Bulletin,* Dec. 1982, pp. 9–13.

Page, J. B. (Chairman, Panel on Alternate Approaches to Graduate Education). *Scholarship for Society.* Princeton, N.J.: Educational Testing Service, 1973.

Parr, S. R. *The Moral of the Story: Literature, Values, and American Education.* New York: Teachers College Press, 1982.

Pell, W. "Facts of Scholarly Publishing." *PMLA,* 1973, *88* (4), 639–644.

Perry, W. G., Jr. *Forms of Intellectual and Ethical Development in the College Years: A Scheme.* New York: Holt, Rinehart and Winston, 1968.

Polanyi, M. *Personal Knowledge.* Chicago: University of Chicago Press, 1958.

Rich, A. "Toward a Woman-Centered University." *Chronicle of Higher Education,* July 21, 1975, p. 32.

Riesman, D. *On Higher Education: The Academic Enterprise in an Era of Rising Student Consumerism.* San Francisco: Jossey-Bass, 1981.

Rogers, C. *Freedom to Learn.* Columbus, Ohio: Merrill, 1969.

Rudolph, F. *Curriculum: A History of the American Undergraduate Course of Study Since 1636.* San Francisco: Jossey-Bass, 1977.

Sanford, N. "Ends and Means in Higher Education." In K. Smith (Ed.), *Current Issues in Higher Education 1962: Higher Education in an Age of Revolutions.* Washington, D.C.: Association for Higher Education, National Education Association, 1962.

Schwab, J. J. *Science, Curriculum, and Liberal Education: Selected Essays.* (I. Westbury and N. J. Wilkof, Eds.) Chicago: University of Chicago Press, 1978.

Schwartz, D. "The Heavy Bear." *In Dreams Begin Responsibilities.* Norfolk, Conn.: New Directions, 1938.

Scully, M. G. "Colleges Urged to Combat 'Civic Illiteracy.'" *Chronicle of Higher Education,* Nov. 25, 1981, pp. 1, 12.

Scully, M. G. "First Major Study Since 1969 Rates Quality of Graduate Programs." *Chronicle of Higher Education,* Sept 29, 1982, p. 8.

Seeley, J. "The University as Slaughterhouse." In *The Great Ideas Today 1969.* New York: Praeger, 1969.

Seldin, P. *Teaching Professors to Teach.* Croton-on-Hudson, N.Y.: Blythe-Pennington, 1977.

Seldin, P. "How American Colleges Evaluate Teaching: Some Surprising Results." Abstracts of contributed papers, Improving University Teaching, Ninth International Conference, Dublin, Ireland, 1983.

Shropshire, W., Jr. (Ed.). *The Joys of Research.* Washington, D.C.: Smithsonian Institution Press, 1981.

Simmons, A. S. "Colleges Must Speak Out on War and Peace." *Chronicle of Higher Education,* June 23, 1982, p. 48.

Skeen, D. "Academic Affairs." *Psychology Today,* 1981, *15,* 100.

Taylor, R. "Within the Halls of Ivy — The Sexual Revolution Comes of Age." *Change,* 1981, *13* (4), 22–29.

Thoreau, H. D. *The Illustrated Walden.* Princeton, N.J.: Princeton University Press, 1973. (Originally published 1854.)

Trotter, R. J. "Decline in Mathematics Skills Worries Scientists." *Chronicle of Higher Education,* Jan. 13, 1982, p. 10.

U.S. Bureau of the Census. *Current Population Reports.* Washington, D.C.: U.S. Government Printing Office, 1982.

Vance, N. S. "Colleges, NCAA Clash Over How to Split Increasingly Big Money for TV Sports." *Chronicle of Higher Education,* Sept. 8, 1982a, pp. 13, 16.

Vance, N. S. "NCAA Names Independent Panel to Find 'Practical Solutions' to Sports Problems." *Chronicle of Higher Education,* August 11, 1982b, pp. 1, 11.

Watkins, B. T. "University of Mid-America Short of Funds, Going Out of Business." *Chronicle of Higher Education,* June 23, 1982, p. 8.

Wehrwein, A. C. "Court Orders U. of Minnesota to Admit Athlete to Degree Program: Excerpts from U.S. Judge's Decision on Minnesota Basketball Player." *Chronicle of Higher Education,* Jan. 13, 1982, p. 5.

Weinberg, A. M. "The Scientific University and the Socio-Technological Institute in the 21st Century." *The Graduate Journal,* 1971, *8* (2), 311–316.

Weiss, S. "I Remember Max." *Chronicle of Higher Education,* Feb. 10, 1982, p. 56.

Whitehead, A. N. *The Aims of Education.* New York: Mentor, 1949. (Originally published 1929).

Whiteley, J. M. *Character Development in College Students.* Vol. 1: *The Freshman Year.* Schenectady. N.Y.: Character Research Press, 1982.

Wiley, J. P., Jr. "Phenomena, Comment and Notes." *Smithsonian,* 1982, *13* (5), 26, 28.

Wilson, R. C., and others. *College Professors and Their Impact on Students.* New York: Wiley, 1975.

Winkler, K. J. "When It Comes to Journals, Is More Really Better?" *Chronicle of Higher Education,* Apr. 14, 1982, pp. 21–22.

Wolfle, D. *The Home of Science: The Role of the University.* New York: McGraw-Hill, 1972.

Wolkomir, R. "A Manic Professor Tries to Close Up the Language Gap." *Smithsonian,* 1980, *11* (2), 80–86.

Index

A

Abramson, R., xiii, 10, 11
Acting, and teaching style, 8–10
Adams, J., 152
Adams, J. T., 152, 174
American Association for Higher Education, xiv
American Association for the Advancement of Science, 82
American Association of University Professors (AAUP), 142, 162, 164, 174
American Council of Learned Societies, 77
American Council on Education, 174
Appearance, and style, 6–8
Arrogance: and insecurity, 104–105; manifestations of, 106–107; about rightness, 106; as sin of teaching, 104–107; about specialization, 104–105; about subject matter, 105–106
Association of American Colleges, Project on the Status and Education of Women, 51
Athletics: and equity for women, 52; and hypocrisy, 117–119; trends in, 166–167
Axelrod, J., xiii, 13, 175

B

Bacon, F., xi, 87, 88, 95–96, 175
Baldwin, R. G., 27, 175
Barzun, J., 124
Bate, W. J., 20, 175
Bauer, H., 63–64
Berry, E., 77
Blackburn, R. T., 27, 71, 175
Bok, S., 24, 175

Boulanger, N., 154
Boyer, E. L., 143, 175
Brockway, G. P., 4-5, 175
Bronowski, J., 22-23, 29, 156, 175
Brown University, and women, 53
Buffon, G. L. L., 2
Buscaglia, L., 38, 175
Bush Foundation, xiv, 122

C

California, University of, size of, 158
California at Berkeley, University of: graduate school rating of, 162; and Lawrence Livermore National Laboratory protest, 24; sexual relationships at, 37
California at Irvine, University of, Sierra Project at, 23-24
Callahan, D., 24, 175
Carlyle, T., 18
Carnegie Commission on Higher Education, 97
Carnegie Foundation for the Advancement of Teaching, 143
Carnegie investigation, 166
Ceci, S. J., 77-78, 175
Centra, J. A., xiii, 123, 130, 136, 175
Chairpersons, and faculty development, 129-130
Character: analysis of, 17-35; breadth and depth related to, 28-31; concept of, 18; and craft, 61; development of in graduate students, 25-28; development of, in undergraduate students, 19-23; and direct approach to values and ethics, 23-25; dynamics of, 19; in higher education, 33-35; and institutional climate, 24-25; and mentoring, 21, 26, 27-28; style and soul related to, 17-19; and values in graduate school, 31-33
Charbonnier, G., 94, 175
Chicago, University of, Committee of Human Development at, 20
Civic responsibility, teaching toward, 143-149

Clark, K., 124
Cole, J. R., 71, 175
Cole, S., 71, 175
Collins, M. J., xiii, 32, 176
Colorado, University of, size limited for, 158
Columbia University: teachers at, 26; university seminars at, 30; women students at, 53
Commission for Undergraduate Education in Biological Sciences (CUEBS), 121
Community, as first principle, 96-97
Corey, I., 1
Costin, F., 136, 176
Cowley, G., 170, 176
Craft: analysis of, 54-63; and character, 61; as guile, 55-57; and honesty, 62-63; and humility, 57-58; learning, 60-61; principles for using, 57; and utility, 58-59
Csikszentmihalyi, M., xiii, 20-21, 45, 46, 100, 176
Cultural ends, teaching toward, 150-153

D

Danforth Associates, 38
Danforth Foundation, xiv, 38
Dante, A., 119
Darwin, C., 29
da Vinci, L., 67-68
Descartes, R., 44
Dickens, C., 109
Discussion, and personal relationships, 40
Dolar, M., 43, 176
Dubos, R., 87, 102, 156, 176
Dullness: defenses of, 108; nature of, 109; as sin of teaching, 107-110

E

Educational Testing Service, xiv
Einstein, A., 75
Epstein, J., 41-42, 142, 154, 176
Erickson, B. L., xiii, 12, 176
Erickson, G. R., 12, 176

F

Faculty development: for beginning teachers, 126–128; and chairpersons, 129–130; efforts at, 121–123; and graduate school experiences, 124–126; and insight into learning, 137–140; limitations of, 134–135; participation in, 123, 127–128; and student evaluations, 135–137; and teaching awards and incentives, 130–134
Faunce, W. H. P., 53, 176
Fink, L. D., 128, 176
Foucalt, M., 102, 176
French-Lazovik, G., xiii, 136–137, 176
Friedrich, R. J., Jr., 121, 177, 178

G

Galileo, G., 29
Gibbon, E., 18
Graduate schools: breadth and depth in, 28–31; character development in, 25–28; ethics courses in, 24; learning to teach in, 124–126; trends in, 162–163; values in,31–33
Granrose, J. T., xiii, 67, 177
Gullette, M. M., 14, 60, 177

H

Hall, R. M., 51, 177
Hampshire College, breadth and depth at, 30
Hardison, O. B., Jr., 75, 177
Harvard-Danforth Center for Teaching and Learning, 60
Harvard University: graduate school rating of, 162, sexual relationships at, 37
Hastings Center, 24, 177
Hawkins, H., 84–85, 177
Hazen Foundation, 113
Hechinger, F., 143, 175
Heilbrun, C. G., 53, 177
Higher education: achievements of, 170–173; aims of, 142–156; anti-intellectualism in, 88; changes and

trends in, 157–173; character of, 33–35; comparative statistics on, 158–159; compassion and cooperation in, 35; cooperation and group effort in, 147–148; democratic paradox in, 144; faculty trends in, 163–164; frivolous inertia in, 155; grimness of, 47–49; limbo, purgatory, and paradise in, 159–163; problems unresolved in, 169–170; purpose of, 122; racial justice in, 34; remedial work in, 167–169; responsibility of, 31–32; sexism in, 50–53; sexual equity in, 34, 53; sexual relationships in, 37–38; student trends in, 164–165; for survival, 148–149, 173
Highet, G., 26, 177
Hildebrand, M., 123, 177
Hill, N. K., 47, 177
Hofstadter, R., 88, 177
Houseman, J., 1
Hypocrisy, as sin of teaching, 117–119

I

Iacocca, L., 165
Insensitivity: and ambition, 112; as incompetence, 113; as sin of teaching, 111–113
Institutional climate: and character, 24–25; for teaching, 140
Ionesco, E., 43–44, 177

J

Jaeger, W., 20, 27, 177
Jaques-Dalcroze, E., 11, 178
Jefferson, T., 87
Johnson, S., 29
Joy, and teaching, 45–49

K

Kafka, F., 18, 93
Katz, C., 53, 178
Knowledge: analysis of questionable value of, 86–102; assumptions about, 89–94; and basic skills

courses, 98–99; as cognitive, 92–93; explosion of, 90–91; furthest end of, 94–96; and interdisciplinary clustering, 97–98; and knowing, 93–94; as quantifiable and structural, 89–91; religious respect for, 86–87; as sequential, 90; as specialized, 91–92; and teaching for survival, 97–102; tenets of faith about, 87–89
Kohlberg, L., 23
Krishne, E. D., 164, 178
Kulik, J. A., 137, 178

L

Lavelle's study, 76
Learning: aspects of, 139; flow experience in, 45–47; indications of, 48–49; insight into, 137–140; rock climbing compared with, 45–47; and trust, 49–50
Lecturing, and personal relationships, 39–40
Letterman, D., 165
Lèvi-Strauss, C., 94
Lilly Foundation, 122
Lindbergh, C., 102
Loevinger, J., 23
Long, F. A., 97–98, 178
Long Beach State University, sexuality course at, 43
Lord, M. W., 118
Lo Schiavo, J., 166
Lucas, F. L., 5, 17, 178

M

McKeachie, W. J., xiii, 60, 137, 178
Magarrell, J., 163, 178
Manhattan College, teacher at, 10
Marsh, H. W., 137, 164, 178
Martin, W. B., 25, 160, 178
Massachusetts Institute of Technology, graduate school rating of, 162
Master's degree, in liberal studies, 30–31
Mathematical literacy, and scholarship-teaching linkage, 82–83

Mencken, H. L., 152
Mentoring, and character, 21, 26, 27–28
Michalak, S. J., Jr., 121, 177, 178
Mid-America, University of, and technology, 171
Miller, J. W., 4–5
Minnesota, University of, and athletics, 118
Modern Language Association, and academic publishing, 75–76
Montaigne, M. E., 29
Moral imagination, in graduate schools, 29
Moral responsibility, teaching toward, 153–156
Morality, and human development, 154
Myers, I. B., 12, 178
Myers-Briggs personality types, 12

N

Nash, 14
National Collegiate Athletic Association (NCAA), 117, 166
National Enquiry into Scholarly Communication, 77
National Science Foundation, 121
Newman, F., 28, 124, 178
Newton, I., 71, 106
Nietzsche, F., 67
Nixon, R., 165

O

Oakeshott, M. J., 94, 178
Ohio State University, size of, 158
Oklahoma, University of, and athletics, 167
Oppenheimer, R., 29
Overall, J. U., IV, 137, 178

P

Page, J. B., 28, 179
Parr, S. R., 32, 33, 179
Pell, W., 75–77, 179
Personality, and style, 5–6, 12–13

Peters, D. P., 77-78, 175
Piaget, J., 23
Pittsburgh, University of, teacher at, 77
Plato, 3
Polanyi, M, 93, 179
Pollack, R., 53
Pope, A., 106, 109-110
Presence: and acquiring a style, 6-8; concept of, 6
Princeton University, teaching at, 4,5
Project to Improve College Teaching, 121

R

Rassias, J., 139
Remedial work, trends in, 167-169
Research, and scholarship, 78-80
Rhode Island, University of, teaching consultants at, 12
Rich, A., 53, 179
Riesman, D., xiii, 165, 178, 179
Rigidity, as sin of teaching, 110-111
Rock climbing, learning compared with, 45-47
Rogers, C., 3-4, 154, 156, 179
Rudolph, F., xiii, 101, 179
Russell, B., 142

S

Sagan, C., 165
San Francisco, University of, and athletics, 166
San Jose State University, sexual relationships at, 37
Sandler, B. R., xiii, 51, 177
Sanford, N., ix-x, 179
Sartre, J.-P., 119
Scholarship: analysis of, 69-85; changing perspectives toward, 84-85; criteria for, 83; interdisciplinary, 80-81; and productivity, 69-75; and publication, 75-78; quality and quantity in, 75-78; and research, 78-80; teaching linked with, 80-83
Scholastic Aptitude Test, 81
Schwab, J. J., 39-40, 179

Schwartz, D., 48, 179
Sciences: and moral responsibility, 155-156; teaching of, 99-100
Scully, M. G., 143, 179
Seeley, J., 102, 179
Seldin, P., 126, 136, 179
Self-indulgence: and collective bargaining, 115; impact of, 116-117; as sin of teaching, 114-117; and sloth, 115-116
Sennett, R., 14
Sex, teaching compared with, 37-41
Sexism, and teaching, 50-53
Shakespeare, W., 33, 43, 79
Shropshire, W., Jr., 75, 180
Simmons, A. S., 30, 180
Skeen, D., 37, 180
Society for Scientific Exploration, 63
Socrates, 37, 41
Soul: character and style related to, 17-19; concept of, 17-18
Southern California, University of, teacher at, 38
Speaking, and style, 9-10
Stanford University, graduate school rating of, 162
Students: changes and trends among, 164-165; character development for, 19-33; evaluation of teaching by, 63, 135-137; love of, 43-44; and teachers unequal, 146-147; values and ethics development among, 23-25
Style: acquiring, and presence, 6-8; and acting, 8-10; analysis of, 1-16; background on, 1; character as foundation of, 17-35; concept of, 2-3; developing, 14-16; didactic or evocative, 13; examples of, 4-5, 7; and faculty behaviors, 15-16; and physical selves, 10-11; responsive, 14; studies of, in teaching, 12-14; as subject or student oriented, 12; in teaching, 3-6; and wisdom, 16
Subject: arrogance about, 105-106; love of, 41-43
Survival: higher education for, 148-149, 173; teaching for, and knowledge, 97-102

T

Taylor, R., 38, 180

Teachers: beginning, development of, 126–128; beginning, study of, 128; change stimulating for, 131–132; citizens separated from, 145–146; as learners, 120–140; love of subject, students, or work by, 41–45; mentoring by, 21, 26, 27–28; perspectives of, toward students, 100; and public schooling, 144–145; responsibilities of, 26–27, 32, 146, 147, 151, 154, 172; senior ranks of, and faculty development, 132–134; and students unequal, 146–147; trends among, 163–164; as "university professors," 133; values of, 32–33

Teaching: and affective domain, 152–153; aims of, 141–156; as art, 66–68; awards and incentives for, 130–134; and campus appearance, 150–151; changing perspectives toward, 84–85; and civic responsibility, 143–149; as craft, 54–63; and cultural ends, 150–153; democratic, 148–149; and discriminating, 153; flight from, 113; and joy, 45–49; joys of, 36–53; learning about, in graduate school, 124–126; and moral responsibility, 153–156; nature of, 54–68; personal relationship in, 38–39; and practical ends, 149–150; and scholarly productivity, 72–75; scholarship in conflict with, 69–85; scholarship linked with, 80–83; as science, 63–66; selectivity in, 101; sex compared with, 37–41; sexism in, 50–53; sins in, 103–119; student evaluation of, 63, 135–137; with style, 1–16; for survival, and knowledge, 97–102; and technology, 64, 171–172; and trust, 49–50

Teaching assistants, and learning to teach, 125–126

Thoreau, H. D., 19, 41, 45, 48, 59, 180

Trotter, R. J., 82, 180

Trust, teaching and learning related to, 49–50

U

United Kingdom: Open University in, 171; training of beginning teachers in, 126

U.S. Bureau of the Census, 164, 180

Utah, University of, student participation at, 164–165

V

Values: direct approach to, 23–25; in graduate school, 31–33

Vance, N. S., 166, 167, 180

Van Doren, M., 26

Vanity, as sin of teaching, 113–114

Vassar College, faculty development at, 10

Virginia Polytechnic Institute, and science, 63

Von Neumann, J., 22

W

Ward, S., 167

Warhol, A., 84

Watkins, B. T., 171, 180

Wehrwein, A. C., 118, 180

Weinberg, A. M., 97, 180

Weiss, S., 4–5, 180

West, M., 77

Whitehead, A. N., xii, 141, 142, 149, 154–155, 180

Whiteley, J. M., ix, 23, 180

Whitman, W., 6

Wiley, J. P., Jr., 63, 180

Williams, College, teacher at, 4

Wilson, R. C., 123, 180

Winkler, K. J., 77, 180

Wolfle, D., 97, 181

Wolkomir, R., 139, 181

Women, effects of sexism on, 51–52

Woolley, D., xiii, 59

Work, love of, 44–45

Writing, and scholarship-teaching linkage, 81–82

Y

Yale University: graduate school rating of, 162; sexual relationships at, 37